VEGETARIAN
TAGINES & COUSCOUS

VEGETARIAN
TAGINES & COUSCOUS

65 delicious recipes for authentic Moroccan food

Ghillie Başan photography by Steve Painter

RYLAND PETERS & SMALL
LONDON • NEW YORK

DESIGN, PROP STYLING AND
PHOTOGRAPHY Steve Painter
EDITOR Rebecca Woods
PRODUCTION Toby Marshall
ART DIRECTOR Leslie Harrington
EDITORIAL DIRECTOR Julia Charles

FOOD STYLIST Lucy McKelvie
FOOD STYLIST'S ASSISTANT Ellie Jarvis
INDEXER Hilary Bird

First published in 2013 by
Ryland Peters & Small
20–21 Jockey's Fields
London WC1R 4BW
and
341 E 116th St
New York, NY 10029

www.rylandpeters.com

10 9 8 7 6 5 4 3

Text © Ghillie Başan 2013
Design and photographs ©
Ryland Peters & Small 2013

Printed in China

ISBN: 978-1-84975-432-3

A CIP record for this book is available from
the British Library.

US Library of Congress CIP data has been
applied for.

NOTES
• All spoon measurements are level unless
otherwise specified.
• All eggs are medium (UK) or large (US), unless
otherwise specified. Uncooked or partially cooked
eggs should not be served to the very old, frail,
young children, pregnant women or those with
compromised immune systems.
• Fruit and vegetables are medium-sized, unless
otherwise stated.
• Chillies are fresh, unless otherwise stated.
• When a recipe calls for the grated zest of citrus
fruit, buy unwaxed fruit and wash well before
using. If you can only find treated fruit, scrub
well in warm soapy water before using.
• Ovens should be preheated to the specified
temperatures. We recommend using an oven
thermometer. If using a fan-assisted oven, adjust
temperatures according to the manufacturer's
instructions.
• To sterilize preserving jars, wash them in hot,
soapy water and rinse in boiling water. Place in
a large saucepan and cover with hot water. With
the saucepan lid on, bring the water to a boil and
continue boiling for 15 minutes. Turn off the heat
and leave the jars in the hot water until just before
they are to be filled. Invert the jars onto a clean
dish towel to dry. Sterilize the lids for 5 minutes,
by boiling or according to the manufacturer's
instructions. Jars should be filled and sealed
while they are still hot.

contents

Moroccan culinary roots

Morocco is one of three countries known collectively as the Maghreb (Morocco, Tunisia and Algeria), perched at the northwest corner of Africa, like a culinary gateway to the native influences of central and northern Africa, to the ancient and medieval traditions of the Arab world to the east, and to the Andalusian flavours of southern Spain across the water. Geographically diverse, Morocco has a little bit of everything – desert, mountains, fertile inner and coastal plains, and an enviable coastline on the Mediterranean and Atlantic oceans – and remarkably for its location it experiences all four seasons, providing the soil with sufficient rain for substantial crops of wheat, maize, vegetables, herbs and fruit.

The indigenous population of Morocco are the Berbers, whose culinary roots have absorbed the influences of early traders, invaders and colonizers: the Phoenicians, who established trading posts along the coast; the Carthaginians in the 5th century BC; the Romans who made the region a Roman province under Emperor Claudius; and the Byzantines when the Roman Empire divided. The 7th-century Arab invasions across the Middle East and North Africa had a big impact on the region, both in a cultural and culinary way, as most of the inhabitants were converted to Islam, the Arabic language, and the restrictions that the religion imposed.

The Arabs also brought the spices of the East, such as ginger, saffron, caraway and cumin, flavours that were quickly absorbed into the traditional cuisine, and they introduced the idea of matching sweet with sour, using honey and fruit, to impart a taste they had adopted from the Persians. It is this sweet

and sour taste, combined with spices, that gives the Moroccan tagines their own distinctive flavour. The Moors who were expelled from Spain introduced olives, olive oil, tomatoes and paprika, and the Jewish refugees fleeing the Spanish Inquisition, brought with them valuable preserving techniques, hence the ubiquitous 'preserved lemons'. The Ottoman Turks also left their mark of sophisticated pastry making and kebabs, and the Spanish and French who colonized sections of Morocco had a lasting influence on the cooking styles, such as soups and sophisticated fish dishes, and on the café culture, wine-making, and the language of the region. Even today, many of the dishes cooked in Morocco are known by their French names.

Moroccan markets

The souks and the old medinas are the lungs of Morocco's culinary culture. Magical and enticing, filled with arresting aromas and colourful displays, they are bustling venues for haggling, meal planning and snacking. Everything you need to make a meal is widely available in the street markets: dried apricots, dates, prunes and figs; roasted pistachios, almonds and walnuts; big bunches of fresh flat leaf parsley, mint and coriander/cilantro; tubs of spices and dried herbs; the distilled waters of rose petals and orange blossom; sacks of flour, grains and couscous; earthenware tagines with their domed or conical lids; and large copper k'dras for celebratory feasts.

It is here that you will also find the seasonal vegetables on display – leeks and carrots the length of baseball bats; aubergines/eggplants like big boxing gloves; juicy tomatoes gleaming like Christmas baubles; globe artichokes on their stems like giant thistles in a vase; and onions, yams, squashes and sweet potatoes in all shapes and sizes. You will also find tiny stalls stacked from floor to ceiling with colourful jars of pickles and preserves; olive sellers displaying every conceivable olive in bowls, jars, wooden vats and earthenware crocks – some salted or preserved in brine, others stuffed or marinated with herbs and spices; and barrels and bottles of pressed olive oil, pumpkin seed and sunflower seed oils, and the precious, dark-red, argan oil, which is highly regarded for both cosmetic and culinary uses. If you travel in the south of Morocco, you may see the extraordinary sight of goats climbing the thorny branches of the stout argan trees to eat the green fruit and, waiting patiently, are the herders who collect their droppings to extract the nuts, which are given to the village women who dry and grind the kernels to produce this rich, nutty oil.

Traditional tagines

A tagine is essentially a glorified, slow-cooked stew, deeply aromatic and full of flavour, although most vegetable tagines don't require long cooking times. The word 'tagine' is both the name of the cooked dish and the cooking vessel. Placed over a charcoal stove, which disperses the heat all around the base, a tagine enables the ingredients to cook gently in the steam that builds up inside the lid, so that they remain beautifully tender and moist. Traditionally a tagine would be served as a course on its own with bread to dip into the sauce, but in many modern homes it is served with couscous. On festive occasions, the classic way of serving a tagine and couscous together is to pile a huge mound of the grains in the shape of a high pyramid and to hollow out the peak to form a dip into which the tagine can be spooned. However, most traditional tagines are not designed for large quantities, so large copper pots are often employed for feasts.

Fluffing the couscous

Couscous is Morocco's national dish. It is of fundamental value to Moroccan culture for dietary, religious and symbolic reasons, as Moroccans believe that it brings God's blessing upon those who consume it. It is therefore prepared in every household on Muslim holy days and on Fridays, the Islamic day of rest, when it is traditionally distributed to the poor as well. There is a Moroccan saying that 'each granule of couscous represents a good deed', so it is not surprising that thousands of granules are consumed in a day.

The word 'couscous' refers to the granules as well as the cooked dish, which is traditionally prepared in a 'couscoussier' – a two-tiered pot with a stewing section at the base and a steaming pot on top for the couscous. Although referred to as a 'grain', it is not technically one; instead it could be described as Moroccan 'pasta' as it is made with semolina flour which is mixed with water and hand-rolled to different sizes. Outside Morocco, the most commonly available packets of couscous are already precooked and only require soaking in water to swell, before being fluffed up and aerated with fingers and oil. The preparation of couscous plays such an important part in Moroccan culinary life that it determines the status of a cook's ability, and fluffing it to perfection can secure a man's hand in marriage.

harissa

This rich, fiery paste is wonderful stuff and is essential to every kitchen in the Maghreb. It is worth making a small batch of your own (a little goes a long way!) to keep handy in the refrigerator as it is a very versatile ingredient. It can be added to many tagines and couscous dishes; it can be served as a condiment to accompany just about anything; it can be stirred into sauces and marinades; and it can be transformed into a dip for warm crusty bread by combining it with oil or yogurt. Prepared by pounding spices and fresh coriander/cilantro with dried red chillies that have been soaked in water, or chillies that have been roasted in oil, harissa imparts a distinct taste to many Moroccan dishes. Jars of ready-prepared harissa are available in North African and Middle Eastern stores, as well as in some larger supermarkets and delicatessens, or you can make your own version based on this recipe. You can try varying it with fennel or caraway seeds, fresh or dried mint, ground black pepper and roasted chillies instead of dried ones.

12 dried red chillies (Horn or New Mexico), deseeded

1 teaspoon cumin seeds

2 teaspoons coriander seeds

1 teaspoon sea salt

3-4 garlic cloves, roughly chopped

a small bunch of fresh coriander/cilantro, finely chopped

4 tablespoons olive oil

a small sterilized jar (see page 4)

MAKES A SMALL JAR

Put the chillies in a bowl and pour over enough warm water to cover them. Leave them to soak for 2–3 hours, then drain and squeeze out any excess water.

Using a mortar and pestle, pound the cumin and coriander seeds to a coarse paste with the salt. Add the garlic and pound until creamy, then add the chillies and pound to a thick paste. Stir in the fresh coriander/cilantro and bind with most of the olive oil.

Transfer the paste to a small sterilized jar and pour in the remaining oil so that there is a thin layer floating on top. It will keep well in the refrigerator for up to 1 month.

2–3 garlic cloves, roughly chopped

1 red chilli, deseeded and roughly chopped

1–2 teaspoons cumin seeds

1 teaspoon sea salt

a big bunch of fresh coriander/cilantro leaves, finely chopped

a pinch of saffron threads, soaked in a little water

freshly squeezed juice of 1 lemon

3–4 tablespoons olive oil

MAKES A BOWL

chermoula

Prepared predominantly with fresh coriander/cilantro, lemon and chillies, chermoula lends its distinct hot, citrus flavour to many marinades, grilled dishes, and vegetable tagines. Unlike the deep, fiery notes of harissa, chermoula is light and lemony with a mild burst of chilli and is best prepared on the day that it will be used.

Using a mortar and pestle, pound the garlic with the chilli, cumin seeds and salt to a coarse paste. Add the chopped coriander/cilantro and pound again to as smooth a paste as you can get. Stir in the saffron, along with its soaking water, and the lemon juice and olive oil.

ras el hanout

This traditional spice mix is so wonderfully pungent and eloquent, it could be described as poetry in a powder. Full of character, reflecting centuries of trade, war, diverse cultures and the geographical spread of Morocco's culinary history, this synthesis of spices is fiery, aromatic and warming all at the same time. Packed with strong Indian aromas of cardamom, cloves, ginger, peppercorns and mace; cinnamon from Sri Lanka; cloves from Zanzibar; local African roots and plants, such as guinea pepper from the Ivory Coast; orris root from the Atlas Mountains; and the delicate, perfumed notes of rose buds, belladonna berries, fennel flowers and lavender from Morocco and Europe, ras el hanout is as unique as the hand that makes it, as every spice merchant has his own recipe. Translated from Arabic as 'head of the shop' it is a delightfully complex medley of 30–40 different spices. Beyond the souks of Morocco, it is difficult to make an authentic ras el hanout, but you can create your own version by loosely following the recipe below, or you can order the aromatic ras el hanout produced by Seasoned Pioneers at www.seasonedpioneers.co.uk.

1 teaspoon black peppercorns	2 teaspoons ground ginger	1 dried red chilli
1 teaspoon cloves	2 teaspoons ground turmeric	1 teaspoon dried lavender
1 teaspoon aniseed seeds	2 teaspoons coriander seeds	6 dried rose buds, broken up
1 teaspoon nigella seeds	2 pieces of mace	
1 teaspoon allspice berries	2 pieces of cinnamon bark	**MAKES 4–5**
1 teaspoon cardamom seeds	2 teaspoons dried mint	**TABLESPOONS**

Using a mortar and pestle, or an electric blender, grind together all the spices to form a coarse powder.

Stir in the dried lavender and rose petals and tip the mix into an airtight container.

You can store the spice mix for about 6 months if you keep it in a cool cupboard well away from direct sunlight.

smen

An acquired taste, smen is an aged butter with a rancid flavour. Often flavoured with herbs and spices and set in earthenware pots, smen can be stored in a cool, dry place for months, sometimes years. It is the primary cooking fat for many Berber communities, who also enjoy this pungent butter smeared on bread. An essential component of many traditional tagines, particularly ones with a high spice content, smen can be substituted with ghee (clarified butter), which isn't as pungent as smen but it does emit a warm, nutty aroma to the dish. Ghee (usually an Indian brand) is sold in Middle Eastern and Asian stores, as well as in some larger supermarkets, or you can try making your own version of smen.

500 g/4 sticks unsalted butter, at room temperature

1 tablespoon sea salt

1 tablespoon dried oregano

a sterilized jar (see page 4)

MAKES ABOUT 500 G/1 LB.

Soften the butter in a bowl. Put the salt and dried oregano in a saucepan with 150 ml/2/3 cup water and boil to reduce it a little. Strain the water directly onto the butter and stir with a wooden spoon to make sure it is well blended, then leave to cool.

Knead the butter with your hands to bind it, squeezing out any excess water. Drain well and spoon the butter into the prepared jar. Seal the jar and store it in a cool, dry place for at least 6 weeks before using in a recipe.

preserved lemons

Small, thin-skinned lemons native to the Maghreb are traditionally preserved in salt and lemon juice to impart a distinctive, citrus flavour to many tagines, grilled dishes and salads. Generally, it is only the rind, finely chopped or sliced, that is employed in the dishes as the flesh is too salty. The refreshing, tangy taste of these preserved lemons is unique and is essential to the cooking of many traditional tagines, particularly vegetable ones. You can buy jars of ready-preserved lemons in Middle Eastern and North African stores, as well as some supermarkets and delicatessens but they are easy to make at home.

10 organic, unwaxed lemons, plus the juice of 3-4 lemons

about 10 tablespoons sea salt

a large sterilized jar (see page 4)

MAKES A LARGE JAR

Wash and dry the lemons and slice one of the ends off each lemon. Stand each lemon on the flattened end and make two vertical cuts three-quarters of the way through them, as if cutting them into quarters but keeping the base intact. Stuff a tablespoon of salt into each lemon and pack them into the prepared jar. Store the jar of lemons in a cool place for 3–4 days to soften the skins.

After this time, press the lemons down into the jar, so they are even more tightly packed. Pour the lemon juice over the salted lemons, until they are completely covered. Seal the jar and store it in a cool place for at least a month.

To use, rinse the salt off the preserved lemons and pat them dry. Using a small sharp knife, cut the lemons into quarters lengthways and remove all the flesh and pith so that you are just left with the rind. Finely slice or chop the rind according to the recipe.

mint tea This is the
national drink of Morocco. It is the preferred
beverage for almost every occasion: for breakfast in the morning;
drunk throughout the day while conducting business; offered as a
symbol of hospitality; prepared for feasts; or served at the end of a
meal to aid digestion. A combination of Chinese Gunpowder green tea and sprigs
of fresh mint, traditionally sweetened with at least four sugar lumps per glass, it is
both refreshing and cleansing and the preparation of it can be an elaborate ceremony.
Traditionally brewed in a fine silver-plated teapot, the tea is poured rhythmically from
a height into a set of fine glasses so that a froth forms on the surface. For an extra dash of
ceremony, a fresh orange blossom or jasmine flower might be floated on top of each glass.

2 teaspoons Chinese Gunpowder
green tea

sugar, to taste

a large bunch of fresh peppermint
and other mint leaves

MAKES A POT

Put the green tea into a teapot with a little
sugar and add a little boiling water. Cover
the pot to keep warm and leave the tea to
steep for 5 minutes. Cram in as many mint
leaves as you can and add the rest of the
sugar, to your preferred sweetness. Top
up the teapot with boiling water, cover it
again and leave the tea to steep for another
5–10 minutes.

Pour a little of the tea into a glass, then
tip it back into the pot, making sure it is
well mixed. Pour the tea into the glasses,
lifting the pot higher and higher and then
lowering it again while pouring, until a thin
layer of bubbly froth forms on the surface
of the tea. Serve immediately.

APPETIZERS
& SOUPS

cracked green olives with cardamom and harissa

Moroccans love olives. In every souk, you will find olive stalls with great vats of varied sizes and shades of green, purple, brown and black, some for eating, others for cooking, and many in marinades of oils, spices, garlic and herbs. Perfect as an appetizer, this recipe offers you a little taste of Morocco in a bowl.

1 teaspoon cumin seeds

1 teaspoon coriander seeds

1-2 teaspoons cardamom seeds

4-6 black peppercorns

2-3 tablespoons olive oil

freshly squeezed juice of ½ lemon

1-2 teaspoons Harissa (see page 12)

350 g/12 oz. (about 2 cups) cracked green olives, rinsed and drained

SERVES 4–6

Dry roast the cumin, coriander and cardamom seeds with the black peppercorns in a skillet, until they emit a nutty aroma. Using a mortar and pestle, crush the roasted spices to a coarse powder. Stir in the olive oil and lemon juice and add the Harissa.

Put the olives into a serving bowl and spoon the spice mixture over them. Toss well and leave to sit for at least 30 minutes before serving.

The olives will keep in a sealed jar in the refrigerator for 3–4 weeks.

dried fruit and nuts with lime and coriander

In the souks of Morocco, sacks and crates of dried nuts and fruit are a common sight as they feature in so many dishes – from savoury snacks, tagines and couscous to salads and sweet dishes. Pan-fried over a camp, or village, fire, the dried fruit and nuts come to life and are best savoured outdoors in the evening sun as an appetizer with a chilled drink.

150 g/1 cup whole almonds

2 tablespoons ghee or smen, or 1 tablespoon olive oil plus 1 tablespoon butter

2 tablespoons macadamia nuts, halved

2 tablespoons cashew nuts, halved

120 g/¾ cup ready-to-eat dried, stoned/pitted apricots, halved

120 g/¾ cup ready-to-eat dried, stoned/pitted dates, halved

1-2 teaspoons finely chopped dried red chilli

grated zest of 1 lime

a small bunch of coriander/ cilantro leaves, finely chopped

sea salt

SERVES 4–6

Put the almonds in a bowl and pour over enough boiling water to cover them. Leave them to steep for 5–10 minutes, then drain and refresh in cold water. Using your fingers, rub the skins off the almonds and halve them.

Heat the ghee in a wide, heavy-based saucepan, stir in the nuts and sauté for 1–2 minutes. Add the apricots and dates and toss the mixture around the pan until the nuts begin to colour. Stir in the chilli and lime zest and cook for a further 1–2 minutes, then toss in the coriander/cilantro.

Drain the mixture on paper towels and tip into a serving bowl or basket. Toss in some salt to taste and serve warm.

crudités with red chilli dukkah dip

A combination of coarsely ground nuts, seeds and spices, dukkah is often used in parts of the Middle East and North Africa as a dip for flatbreads, fresh vegetables or grilled shellfish, or it is sprinkled liberally over grilled meats. The recipe varies from region to region and can be stored in a sealed container for 3–4 weeks. Serve this dish as a nibble with a glass of wine, or as an appetizer to a meal.

2 teaspoons cumin seeds

2 teaspoons coriander seeds

2 tablespoons hazelnuts

2 tablespoons sunflower seeds

1 tablespoon sesame seeds

1 teaspoon sea salt

2 teaspoons fine dried red chilli/hot pepper flakes

4–5 tablespoons olive oil

2 garlic cloves, crushed

freshly squeezed juice of 1 lemon

2 teaspoons runny honey

2 carrots, peeled and cut into sticks

2 celery stalks, cut into sticks

1 (bell) pepper (any colour), deseeded and cut into sticks

sea salt and freshly ground black pepper

SERVES 4–6

In a small heavy-based pan, dry roast the cumin and coriander seeds until they begin to emit a nutty aroma, then tip them onto a plate. Add the hazelnuts to the pan and dry roast until they begin to brown and emit a nutty aroma, then tip them onto the plate with the spices. Finally, dry roast the sunflower and sesame seeds until they, too, begin to emit a nutty aroma and add them to the nuts and spices. Add the salt and, using a mortar and pestle, pound the roasted spices, nuts, seeds and salt to a coarse paste.

Dry roast the dried chilli/hot pepper flakes in the same pan until they begin to darken. Add the olive oil and stir in the crushed garlic until it begins to colour. Pour the flavoured oil over the spice and nut paste and mix well. Beat in the lemon juice and honey and season with salt and pepper to taste.

Tip the dip into a serving bowl and arrange the vegetables around it, to serve.

deep-fried plantains with zahtar

In North and Central Africa, plantains are rarely eaten raw, but they are often cooked as a vegetable in soups and stews, or they are grilled or fried and served as a savoury or sweet dish. Zahtar is a popular spice in the Middle East and North Africa as the combination of dried thyme and sumac goes with almost everything.

2 large, ripe plantains

sunflower oil, for deep frying

1–2 tablespoons zahtar

sea salt

SERVES 4-6

To peel the plantains, chop off the ends, slit the skins lengthways and remove them in strips.

Heat enough oil in a deep saucepan for deep frying. Slice the plantains quite finely and fry in batches until golden brown. Drain them on paper towels, tip them into a serving bowl or basket, and sprinkle liberally with zahtar and sea salt. Serve immediately, while the plantains are still warm.

filo fingers stuffed with feta, olives, and preserved lemon

Deep-fried and baked filo/phyllo pastries are popular as street snacks and starters. They are simple to make and can be prepared ahead of time so that they just need to be cooked at the last minute. When served as an appetizer to a meal, they are often accompanied by pickles, salads and dips.

200 g/7 oz. feta cheese, rinsed and patted dry

2 tablespoons finely chopped stoned/pitted black olives,

1 preserved lemon, rinsed and finely chopped

1 tablespoon dried mint

a small bunch of fresh flat leaf parsley, finely chopped

1 egg

6 sheets of filo/phyllo pastry (thawed if frozen)

sunflower oil, for deep frying

smoked paprika, for dusting

sea salt and freshly ground black pepper

SERVES 4–6

Crumble the feta into a bowl. Add the olives, preserved lemon, mint and parsley and season with salt (if the feta is salty you won't need any extra salt) and pepper. Break the egg into the bowl and stir everything together well.

Lay the sheets of filo/phyllo on a flat surface and cut them into strips about 8–10 cm/3–4 inches wide and 25–30 cm/10–12 inches long. Cover them with a damp cloth to prevent them from drying out. Place a strip in front of you and put a spoonful of the feta mixture just inside one of the short ends. Pull the end over the mixture and pull over both sides to seal in the filling. Roll the pastry up into a tight finger and place it under a damp cloth. Repeat with the rest of the filling and the pastry strips.

Pour enough oil for deep-frying into a deep saucepan and place it over a high heat. Once the oil is hot, fry the fingers in batches over a medium heat until golden brown. Drain them on paper towels and dust with a little smoked paprika, to serve.

roasted carrot dip with herbs

Simple and tasty, this country dish is delicious served warm as a starter with chunks of fresh crusty bread, or with toasted flatbreads. When served as a snack, it is often accompanied by lumps of coarsely crumbled sheep's cheese, marinated olives and pickled vegetables, fruit or chillies.

500 g/1 lb. 2 oz. carrots, peeled and thickly sliced

100 ml/6 tablespoons olive or argan oil

2 garlic cloves, crushed

2 teaspoons cumin seeds

freshly squeezed juice of 1 lemon

a small bunch of fresh flat leaf parsley, finely chopped

a small bunch of fresh dill, finely chopped

a small bunch of fresh mint leaves, finely chopped

sea salt and freshly ground black pepper

SERVES 4

Preheat the oven to 200°C (400°F) Gas 6.

Spread the carrots in an ovenproof dish and pour over the olive oil. Roast in the preheated oven for about 20 minutes. Toss in the crushed garlic and cumin seeds and pop the dish back in the oven for a further 15 minutes, until the carrots are tender but not soft.

Tip the carrots, along with the oil, garlic and cumin, into a bowl and crush them with a potato masher to form a coarse paste. Beat in the lemon juice and most of the herbs. Season with salt and pepper, and spoon the mixture into a serving bowl.

Garnish the dip with the remaining herbs and serve while warm.

smoked aubergine and yogurt dip with harissa

To smoke the aubergines/ eggplants, you need to cook them directly over a gas flame or over a charcoal grill – baking them in the oven will not give you the desired smoky flavour. If using a charcoal grill, the skin of the aubergines/eggplants will toughen on cooking, which enables you to simply slit them open with a knife and scoop out the smoked flesh before you carry on with the recipe below. Serve the dip as an appetizer with chunks of crusty bread or pieces of toasted flatbread.

2 plump aubergines/eggplants

4 tablespoons thick, creamy yogurt

1–2 garlic cloves, crushed

2 teaspoons Harissa (see page 12)

a small bunch of fresh flat leaf parsley, finely chopped

sea salt and freshly ground black pepper

SERVES 4–6

Place the aubergines/eggplants directly over a gas flame and leave them to smoke, turning them from time to time. The skin will begin to char and flake and may even burst in places, but don't worry. When the aubergines/eggplants are soft to touch, turn off the flame and place the aubergines/eggplants in a plastic bag to sweat for 2–3 minutes. Hold each aubergine/eggplant by the stalk under running cold water and gently peel off the charred skin until you are left with the naked bulb-shaped flesh.

Gently squeeze the flesh to remove any excess water, then place it on a chopping board. Chop off the stalk and discard it, then chop the flesh to a pulp and tip it into a mixing bowl. Beat in the yogurt and garlic, stir in the Harissa and half the parsley, and season with salt and pepper to taste.

Spoon the mixture into a serving bowl and garnish with the rest of the parsley to serve.

strained yogurt and cucumber dip with rose petals

For this recipe you can use shop-bought strained yogurt or you can strain it yourself. To do this, place a large piece of muslin/cheesecloth over a bowl and spoon the yogurt into the middle of it. Gather the ends of the muslin/cheesecloth, tie them together and hook it over the kitchen tap/faucet, or a hook on a shelf, so that the yogurt is suspended over the sink or a bowl, and leave it to drain for 2–6 hours, until it is the consistency of cream cheese. Serve the dip as an appetizer with chunks of fresh crusty bread.

1 cucumber

250 g/1 cup strained yogurt

2 garlic cloves, crushed

2 tablespoons walnuts, roughly chopped

a small bunch of fresh mint leaves,
finely chopped

sea salt and freshly ground black pepper

½ teaspoon dried mint, to garnish

a handful of fresh or dried rose petals,
to garnish

SERVES 4–6

Using a peeler, partially peel the cucumber in strips, leaving
about half of the skin on (which will add texture to the dip).
Discard the peeled skin and grate the cucumber. Spread the
grated cucumber on a plate, sprinkle with salt, and leave it
to weep for 10 minutes.

Put the strained yogurt into a bowl and beat in the garlic,
walnuts and mint leaves. Gather the grated cucumber in your
hands and squeeze it tightly over the sink to get rid of the
excess water and salt. Add the squeezed cucumber to the
yogurt, mix well, and season with salt and pepper.

Spoon the yogurt into a serving bowl and garnish with
a sprinkling of dried mint and the rose petals.

chunky tomato soup with vermicelli and ras el hanout

Some traditional soups are hearty affairs and designed to be enjoyed as a meal on their own. Served with thick, creamy yogurt and chunks of fresh crusty bread, there is really no need for anything else but, if serving the soup as an appetizer to a meal, it would be prudent to omit the bread and follow with a light vegetable couscous.

2–3 tablespoons olive or argan oil

4 garlic cloves, finely chopped

2 onions, chopped

2 celery stalks, chopped

1 carrot, peeled and chopped

8 large, ripe tomatoes, skinned and roughly chopped

1–2 teaspoons sugar

1 tablespoon tomato purée/paste

1–2 teaspoons Ras el Hanout (see page 15)

a big bunch of fresh coriander/cilantro, finely chopped

1.5 litres/6 cups vegetable stock

120 g/4 oz. fine vermicelli, broken into little pieces

sea salt and freshly ground black pepper

2–3 tablespoons thick, creamy yogurt, to serve

SERVES 4

Heat the oil in a heavy-based saucepan and stir in the garlic, onions, celery and carrot, until they begin to colour. Add the tomatoes and the sugar and cook over a medium heat, until the mixture is thick and pulpy.

Stir in the tomato purée/paste, Ras el Hanout, and most of the coriander/cilantro, then pour in the stock and bring the liquid to the boil. Reduce the heat and cook gently for about 15 minutes. Season the soup with salt and pepper to taste, stir in the vermicelli and continue to cook gently until the vermicelli is just tender.

Ladle the soup into individual bowls, swirl a little yogurt into each one, and garnish with the reserved coriander/cilantro, to serve.

creamy pumpkin soup with ginger and chilli honey

Smooth, creamy soups are a legacy of the French but, with the Moroccan penchant for sweet and fiery tastes, the addition of chilli and honey make this soup quite unique. It is a great winter soup and, if it's not a pumpkin time of year, you can use butternut squash instead.

3 tablespoons olive oil

1 tablespoon butter

1 onion, chopped

50 g/a 2-inch piece of fresh ginger, peeled and chopped

2 teaspoons coriander seeds

2 teaspoons fennel seeds

1 kg/2 lbs. 4 oz. peeled and deseeded pumpkin flesh, roughly chopped

1 litre/4 cups vegetable stock

150 ml/⅔ cup double/heavy cream

2–3 tablespoons runny honey

1–2 teaspoons finely chopped dried red chilli

SERVES 4–6

Heat the oil and butter in a heavy-based saucepan, stir in the onion, ginger, coriander seeds and fennel seeds and sauté for 2–3 minutes, until the onion begins to colour. Toss in the pumpkin, stirring to coat it in the onion and ginger, then pour in the stock. Bring the stock to the boil, then reduce the heat, cover the pan and cook gently for about 25 minutes, until the pumpkin is very tender.

Purée the soup with a stick blender, or whiz it in an electric blender, and tip it back into the pan. Simmer the soup over a low heat, season well with salt and pepper and stir in the cream.

Heat the honey in a small pan and stir in the chopped chilli.

Ladle the soup into individual bowls, swirl a little of the chilli honey onto the surface of each one and serve immediately.

saffron, chilli and herb broth

**This type of light broth is often served at the start of a long
meal involving numerous dishes, or as a palate cleanser
between courses. The saffron lends the broth an air of
distinction and colour, the chilli whets the appetite, and the
herbs and spices cleanse and balance the ensuing flavours.**

Pour the stock into a saucepan and add the rest of the ingredients.
Bring the stock to the boil, reduce the heat, and cook gently for
about 1 hour. Taste the soup to adjust the seasoning.

Ladle, or strain, the soup into bowls and serve piping hot.

1 litre/4 cups vegetable stock

2–3 dried red chillies

2 teaspoons cumin seeds

2 teaspoons coriander seeds

1 teaspoon saffron threads

a large bunch of fresh flat leaf parsley
leaves, pulled apart

a large bunch of fresh coriander/cilantro
leaves, pulled apart

a small bunch of fresh mint leaves, whole

4–6 peppercorns

1 teaspoon sea salt

SERVES 4–6

chilled almond and garlic soup

In Tangier and Casablanca, the French and Spanish influence is very evident in the cuisine, such as this chilled soup. Like gazpacho, it is refreshing served on a hot day and, when served as an appetizer to a meal, it whets the appetite for the ensuing courses.

150 g/1 cup blanched almonds, roughly chopped

3–4 slices of stale white bread, crusts removed

4 garlic cloves, roughly chopped

4 tablespoons olive oil

1–2 tablespoons white wine or cider vinegar

sea salt

a small bunch of seedless green or red grapes, finely sliced, to garnish

1 green chilli, deseeded and finely sliced, to garnish

SERVES 4

Put the almonds in a food processor and blend them to a paste. Add the bread and garlic and drizzle in the olive oil, blending all the time. Gradually pour in 850 ml/3½ cups water, blending continuously, until the mixture is smooth like pouring cream. Add the vinegar and season with salt.

Pour the soup into a bowl and chill in the refrigerator for at least 1 hour. Ladle the soup into bowls – adding ice cubes if you wish – and garnish with the grapes and chilli.

LIGHTER
TAGINES

roasted cherry tomato tagine with feta and preserved lemon

Simple and tasty, this tagine offers a great way of cooking cherry or baby plum tomatoes. It can be served as a snack with flatbreads or chunks of crusty bread, or as an accompaniment to grilled and roasted dishes. It is also delicious without the feta, so vegans can enjoy this dish too.

450 g/1 lb. cherry tomatoes

2 tablespoons olive or argan oil

4 garlic cloves, halved and smashed

1 teaspoon sugar

1–2 teaspoons finely chopped dried or fresh chillies

1–2 teaspoons dried oregano

1 Preserved Lemon (see page 16), finely chopped

sea salt

120 g/4 oz. feta cheese

SERVES 4

Preheat the oven to 200°C (400°F) Gas 6.

Tip the cherry tomatoes into the base of a tagine or into a heavy-based casserole and drizzle with the oil. Scatter the smashed garlic around the tomatoes, then sprinkle the sugar, chillies and nearly all of the oregano over the top. Give the tagine a good shake, then place it in the preheated oven for 20–25 minutes, until the tomato skins begin to buckle.

Remove the tagine from the oven and toss in half of the Preserved Lemon. Season with salt, sprinkle the rest of the oregano over the top and pop the tagine back in the oven for 5–10 minutes.

Crumble the feta over the top and garnish with the remaining Preserved Lemon before serving.

roasted aubergine, tomato and chickpea tagine with yogurt

This delicious tagine has unmistakable Middle Eastern and Turkish notes influenced by the nation's history of invasion. Served with toasted flatbreads and a salad, this tagine is both warming and nourishing.

2-3 tablespoons ghee or smen, or 1 tablespoon olive oil plus 1 tablespoon butter

2 teaspoons cumin seeds

2-3 cinnamon sticks

2 aubergines/eggplants, diced

2-3 garlic cloves, crushed

1-2 dried red chillies, finely chopped

8-10 cherry or baby plum tomatoes, halved

1-2 teaspoons sugar

2 teaspoons dried thyme

a 400-g/14-oz. can chickpeas, drained and rinsed

1 Preserved Lemon (see page 16), finely chopped

2-3 tablespoons thick, creamy yogurt

freshly squeezed juice of ½ lemon

sea salt and freshly ground black pepper

dried mint, to garnish

SERVES 4

Preheat the oven to 200°C (400°F) Gas 6.

Heat the ghee in the base of a tagine or in a heavy-based casserole, stir in the cumin seeds and cinnamon sticks and sauté for 1–2 minutes. Toss in the aubergines/eggplants, cover and transfer the tagine to the preheated oven. Roast for 25–30 minutes, turning the aubergines/eggplants once or twice in the ghee and spices during cooking, until tender and golden brown.

Remove the tagine from the oven and toss in the garlic, chilli and tomatoes. Sprinkle the sugar over the top, then return the tagine to the oven for a further 15 minutes. Remove from the oven again, toss in the thyme, chickpeas and Preserved Lemon, and season well with salt and pepper. Return the tagine to the oven for 10 minutes.

In a bowl, beat together the yogurt and lemon juice. Drizzle the yogurt over the tagine, then sprinkle a little dried mint over the top to garnish before serving.

tagine of spicy roasted pumpkin wedges with lime

This is a tasty way of enjoying pumpkin. These spicy wedges can be served as an accompaniment to other tagines, or on their own with a spicy couscous and a salad. Save the seeds and roast them lightly with a little oil and coarse salt to serve as a quick snack.

1 small or ½ medium-sized pumpkin

2 teaspoons coriander seeds

1 teaspoon cumin seeds

1 teaspoon fennel seeds

1–2 teaspoons ground cinnamon

2 dried red chillies, finely chopped

1 teaspoon sea salt

2 garlic cloves, crushed

2–3 tablespoons olive or pumpkin seed oil

1–2 tablespoons honey

1–2 limes, cut into wedges, to serve

SERVES 4–6

Preheat the oven to 200°C (400°F) Gas 6.

Cut the pumpkin in half lengthways and scoop out the seeds with a spoon. Slice each pumpkin half into 4–6 thin wedges, like crescent moons, and arrange them, skin-side down, in a circle in the base of a wide tagine or in a heavy-based casserole.

Using a mortar and pestle, grind all the dried spices with the salt. Add the garlic and enough oil to form a paste. Rub the spicy paste over the pumpkin wedges and drizzle the rest of the oil over them.

Pop the tagine in the preheated oven and roast the pumpkin wedges for 35–40 minutes, until tender. Drizzle the honey over the wedges and return to the oven for a further 10 minutes. Sprinkle a little salt over the pumpkin wedges and serve hot with the lime to squeeze over them.

onion, olive and egg tagine with zahtar

Popular bus station and working men's café fare, this dish can be cooked just as easily in a shallow, heavy-based pan as it is very quick and simple. Served with toasted flatbreads and pickles, it makes a great snack for brunch or lunch.

1 tablespoon olive or argan oil

20 g/1½ tablespoons butter

2 onions, finely sliced

2 garlic cloves, finely chopped

½ teaspoon sugar

1 scant teaspoon finely chopped dried chillies, cayenne or chilli powder

1 tablespoon stoned/pitted and finely sliced black olives

4–6 eggs

1–2 teaspoons zahtar

sea salt and freshly ground black pepper

SERVES 4–6

Heat the oil and butter in the base of a tagine or in a heavy-based saucepan, stir in the onions, garlic and sugar and sauté for 3–4 minutes, until the onion has softened and turned golden brown. Stir in the chillies and the olives, allow them to cook for 1 minute, then season with a little salt and pepper.

Push the olive and onion mixture aside to create 4–6 pockets and crack the eggs into them. Put the lid on the tagine and cook gently for 4–5 minutes, until the whites of the eggs are firm. Sprinkle the zahtar over the top and serve.

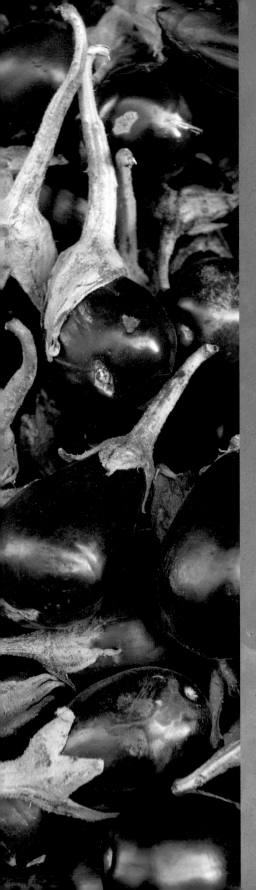

baby aubergine tagine with coriander and mint

This is a tasty way of cooking the baby aubergines/eggplants that are often available in Middle Eastern, North African and Asian stores. However, if you can't find them you can use the slender aubergines/eggplants cut into quarters. Serve this dish with Plain Buttery Couscous (see page 104).

2 tablespoons ghee, or argan or olive oil

1 onion, finely chopped

2–3 garlic cloves, finely chopped

2 red chillies, deseeded and finely chopped

2 teaspoons coriander seeds

2 teaspoons cumin seeds

2 teaspoons sugar

1–2 teaspoons ground fenugreek

8 baby aubergines/eggplants, with stalks intact

2 x 400-g/14-oz. cans chopped tomatoes

a bunch of fresh mint leaves, roughly chopped

a bunch of fresh coriander/cilantro, roughly chopped

sea salt and freshly ground black pepper

SERVES 4

Heat the ghee in the base of a tagine or in a heavy-based saucepan. Stir in the onion, garlic, chillies, coriander and cumin seeds and sugar and sauté for 2–3 minutes, until the onion begins to colour.

Toss in the fenugreek and the aubergines/eggplants, rolling them in the onion and spice mixture. Tip in the tomatoes, bubble them up, put on the tagine lid and cook over a gentle heat for about 40 minutes, until the baby aubergines/eggplants are very tender.

Season the tagine with salt and pepper and toss in most of the mint and coriander/cilantro. Put the lid back on and cook over a medium heat for a further 5 minutes. Garnish with the rest of the mint and coriander/cilantro and serve hot.

baby courgette tagine with courgette flowers and lemon

A unique spring and early summer dish, this tagine is made with baby courgettes/zucchini and the lovely bright yellow flowers of the plant. It is light and lemony and can be served as a first course, as a salad, or as a simple tagine with a little bit of fresh crusty bread to mop up the juices.

2 tablespoons olive or argan oil

2 teaspoons coriander seeds

2 garlic cloves, finely chopped

1 onion, finely chopped

12 baby courgettes/zucchini, trimmed and left whole

1 Preserved Lemon (see page 16), finely sliced

freshly squeezed juice of 2 lemons

4–8 courgette/zucchini flowers, trimmed and left whole

1 tablespoon orange blossom water

sea salt and freshly ground black pepper

a few fresh mint leaves, finely shredded, to garnish

SERVES 4

Heat the oil in the base of a tagine or in a heavy-based saucepan, stir in the coriander seeds, garlic and onion and sauté for 1–2 minutes. Toss in the baby courgettes/zucchini, coating them in the onion and garlic, then add the Preserved Lemon and lemon juice. Put the lid on the tagine and cook gently for 10–15 minutes, until the courgettes/zucchini are tender but still have a bite to them.

Season the tagine with salt and pepper, toss in the courgette/zucchini flowers and splash in the orange blossom water. Put the lid back on and cook gently for 4–5 minutes, until the flowers have wilted in the steam.

Garnish with the shredded mint leaves and serve hot, or at room temperature.

okra and tomato tagine with lemon

It is important to know how to prepare okra before cooking so that they retain their colour and bite, otherwise they can become quite mushy and gelatinous. First, the okra need to be trimmed by cutting off the stalks; then place them in a bowl and toss them well in 2–3 teaspoons salt and 2–3 tablespoons white wine or cider vinegar. Leave the okra to sit for at least 2 hours, then rinse, drain and pat them dry before using. Serve this tagine with plain or spicy couscous.

2 tablespoons olive or argan oil

1 onion, halved lengthways and finely sliced

2 garlic cloves, finely chopped

1–2 red chillies, deseeded and finely chopped

1–2 teaspoons sugar

2 teaspoons coriander seeds

500 g/1 lb. 2 oz. fresh okra, rinsed and prepared as above

freshly squeezed juice of 1 lemon

a 400-g/14-oz. can chopped tomatoes

sea salt and freshly ground black pepper

½ Preserved Lemon (see page 16), finely sliced, to garnish

SERVES 4

Heat the oil in the base of a tagine or in a heavy-based saucepan. Stir in the onion, garlic, chilli, sugar and coriander seeds and sauté for 2–3 minutes. Toss in the okra and add the lemon juice. Tip in the tomatoes, bubble them up, put the lid on the tagine and cook over a medium heat for 15 minutes, until the okra is tender.

Season the tagine with salt and pepper, garnish with the Preserved Lemon, and serve.

three pepper tagine with eggs and ras el hanout

This is one of the typical street tagines served up at market stalls, bus stations, busy ports and working men's cafés. Quick and cheerful, it can be prepared for a snack at any time of day, or for a light meal with toasted flatbreads and garlic-flavoured yogurt.

2 tablespoons ghee or olive oil

1 onion, halved lengthways and sliced

1 teaspoon cumin seeds

1 teaspoon sugar

3 (bell) peppers (green, red and yellow), deseeded and sliced

1–2 teaspoons Ras el Hanout (see page 15), plus a little extra for sprinkling

4 eggs

4 generous tablespoons thick, creamy yogurt

2 garlic cloves, crushed

sea salt and freshly ground black pepper

a small bunch of fresh flat leaf parsley, finely chopped, to garnish

SERVES 4

Heat the ghee in the base of a tagine or in a heavy-based saucepan, stir in the onion, cumin seeds and sugar and sauté for 1–2 minutes. Add the peppers and cook over a medium heat for a further 2–3 minutes, until they have softened. Stir in the Ras el Hanout and season with salt and pepper.

Push the peppers to the sides of the tagine to make room for the eggs. Crack the eggs into the middle of the tagine and dust them with a little Ras el Hanout. Put the lid on the tagine and cook the eggs over gentle heat for 3–4 minutes, until the whites are just firm.

In a mixing bowl, beat the yogurt with the garlic until smooth and season it with salt and pepper to taste. Garnish the tagine with the parsley, divide the eggs and peppers onto 4 plates, and serve with a spoonful of the garlic-flavoured yogurt.

runner bean tagine with tomato and dill

This simple fresh bean tagine is best enjoyed on its own with chunks of fresh crusty bread and thick, creamy yogurt. Be quite liberal with the dill as it is the only flavouring in the tagine and transforms a traditional bean and tomato dish into something deliciously unique.

2 tablespoons olive or argan oil

1–2 onions, roughly chopped

2 garlic cloves, roughly chopped

500 g/1 lb. 2 oz. fresh runner (stringless) beans, trimmed and cut into 3 or 4 pieces

2 teaspoons sugar

freshly squeezed juice of 1 lemon

2 x 400-g/14-oz. cans chopped tomatoes

a bunch of fresh dill, roughly chopped

sea salt and freshly ground black pepper

a small bunch of fresh flat leaf parsley, roughly chopped, to garnish

SERVES 4–6

Heat the oil in the base of a tagine or in a heavy-based saucepan, stir in the onions and garlic and sauté for 2–3 minutes, until the onions soften. Toss in the beans, coating them in the onions and oil, then stir in the sugar and lemon juice. Add the tomatoes and dill, cover with the lid, and cook over gentle heat for about 40 minutes, until the beans are tender and the tomato sauce is fairly thick.

Season the tagine with salt and pepper and garnish with the parsley before serving.

4 artichoke bottoms

125 ml/½ cup olive oil

freshly squeezed juice of 1 lemon

150 g/1 cup blanched almonds

150 g/1 cup ready-to-eat dried apricots, halved or quartered

a 400-g/14-oz. can broad/fava or butter beans, drained and rinsed

1–2 teaspoons sugar

a small bunch of fresh dill, roughly chopped

sea salt and freshly ground black pepper

SERVES 4

tagine of artichokes, broad beans, apricots and almonds

Light and cheerful, this is a lovely tagine to make in the spring or early summer when the globe artichokes are young and tender. You can use fresh artichokes, trimmed to their bottoms, or the frozen ready-prepared bottoms available in some supermarkets. Serve with couscous or a salad.

Put the artichoke bottoms, hollow-side up, in the base of a tagine or in a heavy-based saucepan.

Mix together the olive oil, lemon juice and 50 ml/3 tablespoons water and pour it over the artichokes. Put the lid on the tagine and cook the artichokes for 15–20 minutes over gentle heat, until tender.

Add the almonds, apricots and beans to the tagine. Sprinkle the sugar over them and scatter some of the dill over the top. Put the lid back on and cook gently for a further 10 minutes.

Season the tagine with salt and pepper. Spoon the almonds, apricots and beans into the middle of each artichoke bottom, garnish with the rest of the dill, and serve.

artichokes with ginger, honey and preserved lemon

2 tablespoons olive oil

2 garlic cloves, crushed

25 g/a 1-inch piece of fresh ginger, peeled and finely chopped

1 teaspoon fennel seeds

a pinch of saffron threads, soaked in a little water

freshly squeezed juice of ½ lemon

1–2 tablespoons honey

6–8 artichoke hearts, halved, or artichoke bottoms, cut into quarters

1 Preserved Lemon (see page 16), finely sliced

a small bunch of fresh coriander/cilantro, finely chopped

sea salt and freshly ground black pepper

SERVES 4

For this recipe, you can use fresh globe artichokes, preserved artichoke hearts or frozen artichoke bottoms. To prepare fresh globe artichokes, first remove the outer leaves and cut off the stems. Then, using a teaspoon, scoop out the choke and all the hairy bits. Trim the hearts and bottoms and immerse them in water mixed with a squeeze of lemon juice to prevent them from blackening. Serve the tagine with a lemon, spicy or fruity couscous.

Heat the oil in the base of a tagine or in a heavy-based saucepan, stir in the garlic, ginger and fennel seeds and sauté for 1–2 minutes. Add the saffron, along with its soaking water, lemon juice and honey and simmer gently over a low heat.

Drain the artichokes and add them to the tagine, tossing them in the spices and honey. Add just enough water (roughly 150 ml/⅔ cup) to cover the base of the tagine and stir in most of the Preserved Lemon. Put the lid on the tagine and cook gently for about 15–20 minutes, until the artichokes are tender.

Season the tagine with salt and pepper and toss in most of the coriander/cilantro. Garnish with the rest of the Preserved Lemon and coriander/cilantro to serve.

stuffed prune tagine with walnuts and rosewater

The Romans got as far as Morocco and left many signs of their existence, including the production of wine, which the colonizing French took to new heights. There are several good wines produced in Morocco and occasionally wine is used in cooking, particularly by creative chefs in the restaurants of Rabat and Casablanca. Serve the tagine on its own between courses, or with buttery couscous, crumbled feta and pickled chillies.

16 ready-to-eat dried stoned/pitted prunes

16 walnut halves

1–2 tablespoons ghee, or 1 tablespoon olive oil plus 1 tablespoon butter

2 cinnamon sticks

1 teaspoon cardamom seeds

3–4 cloves

pared peel of ½ orange

250 ml/1 cup red wine

1 tablespoon pomegranate syrup

1 tablespoon honey

1–2 tablespoons rosewater

sea salt and freshly ground black pepper

a small bunch of fresh flat leaf parsley, roughly chopped, to garnish

SERVES 4

Find the opening in each pitted prune and stuff it with a walnut half.

Melt the ghee in the base of a tagine or in a heavy-based saucepan, add the cinnamon sticks, cardamom seeds, cloves and orange peel and sauté for a minute, until fragrant. Add the stuffed prunes to the tagine, turning them over in the spices and ghee, then pour in the red wine. Put the lid on the tagine and cook gently for 15 minutes.

Stir in the pomegranate syrup and the honey. Season the tagine with salt and pepper, put the lid back on and cook gently for another 10 minutes, until the juices begin to caramelize.

Splash in the rosewater, garnish with the parsley, and serve.

tagine of roasted pear with figs, walnuts and cardamom

Sweet, fruity and spicy – this unusual tagine has the hallmarks of an early Arab, or Persian, dish. It is delicious served alongside other tagines and with spicy couscous, or it can be served as a course on its own to balance the palate between spicy dishes.

1-2 tablespoons ghee or argan oil, or 1 tablespoon olive oil plus
1 tablespoon butter

1-2 teaspoons cardamom seeds

4 small pears, peeled, cored and cut into quarters

8–12 ready-to-eat dried figs, halved

175 g/1 generous cup walnut halves

1 dried red chilli, finely chopped

2 tablespoons honey

a small bunch of fresh coriander/cilantro leaves, finely chopped

sea salt and freshly ground black pepper

1 lemon or lime, cut into wedges, to serve

SERVES 4

Preheat the oven to 200°C (400°F) Gas 6.

Heat the ghee in the base of a tagine or in a heavy-based casserole, stir in the cardamom seeds and sauté for 1 minute. Add the pears and toss them to coat in the spices, then put the tagine in the preheated oven for 15 minutes, turning the pears once during cooking.

Take the tagine out of the oven and toss in the dried figs, walnuts and chilli. Drizzle the honey over the pears and return the tagine to the oven for about 15 minutes, until the pears begin to caramelize.

Season the tagine with salt and pepper and toss in most of the coriander/cilantro. Garnish the tagine with the rest of the coriander/cilantro and serve with wedges of lemon or lime.

tagine of butter beans, cherry tomatoes and black olives

This is a delightfully sophisticated tagine, probably a legacy of the French, as it manages to combine three main ingredients with the essential Moroccan flavours of salty, fruity and fiery. You can serve this tagine as a side dish or as a main dish with a leafy salad.

200 g/1⅓ cups dried butter beans, soaked overnight in plenty of water

2-3 tablespoons olive oil

4 garlic cloves, halved and smashed

2 onions, sliced

2 green chillies, deseeded and finely sliced

25 g/a 1-inch piece of fresh ginger, peeled and finely chopped

2 teaspoons coriander seeds

1-2 teaspoons sugar

a pinch of saffron threads, soaked in a little water

about 12 cherry tomatoes

about 12 black olives, stoned/pitted

1-2 teaspoons dried thyme

freshly squeezed juice of 1 lemon

sea salt and freshly ground black pepper

a small bunch of fresh flat leaf parsley, roughly chopped, to garnish

lemon wedges, to serve

SERVES 4–6

Drain and rinse the soaked beans. Put them in a deep pan with plenty of water and bring it to the boil for about 5 minutes. Reduce the heat and simmer gently for about an hour, or until the beans are tender but not mushy. Drain and refresh the beans under running cold water.

Heat the oil in the base of a tagine or in a heavy-based saucepan. Add the garlic, onions, chillies, ginger, coriander seeds and sugar and sauté for 2–3 minutes. Stir in the saffron, along with its soaking water, and toss in the beans. Add the tomatoes, olives, dried thyme and lemon juice, cover with the lid and cook over a gentle heat for 15–20 minutes.

Season the tagine with salt and pepper, garnish with the parsley and serve with wedges of lemon to squeeze over the tagine.

HEARTY
TAGINES

chickpea and spinach tagine with yogurt

This village tagine is usually served with freshly griddled flatbreads, or a warm crusty loaf. If you use canned chickpeas and steam the spinach ahead of time, the tagine takes only 15–20 minutes – ideal for a quick lunch or supper.

Heat the ghee in the base of a tagine or in a heavy-based saucepan, add the onion, garlic, ginger and cumin seeds and sauté until they begin to colour. Toss in the chickpeas, coating them in the onion mixture, and stir in the ground turmeric and Ras el Hanout. Add the spinach and 150 ml/⅔ cup water. Put the lid on the tagine and cook over gentle heat for 10–15 minutes.

Season the tagine with salt and pepper, swirl in the yogurt, dust with the paprika and serve immediately.

1 tablespoon ghee, smen or argan oil, or 1 tablespoon olive oil plus 1 tablespoon butter

1 onion, finely chopped

2 garlic cloves, finely chopped

25 g/a 1-inch piece of fresh ginger, peeled and finely chopped

1 teaspoon cumin seeds

250 g/1⅔ cups cooked chickpeas

1 teaspoon ground turmeric

1–2 teaspoons Ras el Hanout (see page 15)

500 g/1 lb. 2 oz. spinach, steamed and roughly chopped

2–3 tablespoons thick, creamy yogurt

½ teaspoon paprika

sea salt and freshly ground black pepper

SERVES 3–4

cauliflower and chickpea tagine with harissa and preserved lemon

This hearty tagine is typical of the type of dish cooked in the wooded Middle Atlas region and the lush valleys leading up to the High Atlas. It's a tasty way of preparing cauliflower, broccoli or cabbage, and is often simply served with chunks of bread to mop up the sauce.

2 tablespoons ghee, smen or argan oil, or
1 tablespoon olive oil plus 1 tablespoon butter

1 onion, coarsely chopped

2 garlic cloves, coarsely chopped

2 teaspoons coriander seeds

1–2 teaspoons sugar

a 400-g/14-oz. can chickpeas, rinsed and drained

1 cauliflower, trimmed into small florets

a 400-g/14-oz. can chopped tomatoes

2–3 teaspoons Harissa (see page 12)

a bunch of fresh coriander/cilantro, roughly chopped

1 Preserved Lemon (see page 16), finely chopped

sea salt and freshly ground black pepper

SERVES 4–6

Heat the ghee in the base of a tagine or in a heavy-based saucepan, add the onion and sauté for 2–3 minutes to soften. Add the garlic, coriander seeds and sugar and cook for a further 2–3 minutes, until the onion and garlic begin to colour, then toss in the chickpeas and cauliflower florets.

Add the chopped tomatoes, stir in the Harissa and pour in just enough water to cover the cauliflower. Bring the liquid to the boil, reduce the heat, put on the lid, and cook the tagine gently for about 20 minutes, until the cauliflower is tender.

Season the tagine well with salt and pepper, toss in half the coriander/cilantro and Preserved Lemon, and cook for a further 5–10 minutes.

Garnish with the remaining coriander/cilantro and Preserved Lemon and serve.

450 g/1 lb. dried haricot beans, soaked overnight and drained

2–3 tablespoons ghee, smen or argan oil, or 1 tablespoon olive oil plus 1 tablespoon butter

2 onions, finely chopped

4 garlic cloves, finely chopped

2 red chillies, deseeded and finely chopped

2 teaspoons sugar

2 teaspoons Harissa (see page 12)

2 x 400-g/14-oz. cans chopped tomatoes

a bunch of fresh mint leaves, finely chopped

a bunch of fresh flat leaf parsley, finely chopped

a bunch of fresh coriander/cilantro, finely chopped

sea salt and freshly ground black pepper

1–2 lemons, cut into wedges, to serve

SERVES 4–6

bean tagine with harissa and coriander

This is a classic Berber tagine, which can be found in infinite variations throughout Morocco using different beans – haricot, borlotti, black-eyed, broad/fava or butter beans. Often this dish is served on its own with chunks of bread, but it is also delicious served with thick, creamy yogurt and a Moroccan fruit chutney.

Put the beans in a saucepan with plenty of water and bring to the boil. Reduce the heat and simmer for about 30 minutes until the beans are tender. Drain thoroughly.

Heat the ghee in the base of a tagine or in a heavy-based saucepan, add the onions, garlic, chillies and sugar and sauté for 2–3 minutes, until they begin to colour. Stir in the Harissa and toss in the drained beans. Add the tomatoes and top up with a little water to make sure the beans are submerged. Bring the liquid to the boil, reduce the heat, put on the lid and cook gently for about 30 minutes.

Season the tagine with salt and pepper to taste, stir in most of the herbs and simmer for a further 10 minutes. Garnish with the remaining herbs and serve hot with the wedges of lemon to squeeze over the tagine.

lentil tagine with ginger and ras el hanout

Packed with flavour, this spicy lentil tagine is best served on its own with a dollop of thick, creamy yogurt, a Moroccan fruit chutney and toasted flatbread. From the chill air of the Atlas Mountains, this tagine is designed to warm you from within.

2 tablespoons ghee or smen,
or 1 tablespoon olive oil plus
1 tablespoon butter

1 onion, finely chopped

40 g/a 2-inch piece of fresh ginger,
peeled and finely chopped

4 garlic cloves, finely chopped

1–2 teaspoons sugar

2 teaspoons cumin seeds

1 teaspoon coriander seeds

2–3 teaspoons Ras el Hanout
(see page 15)

300 g/1½ cups brown lentils, rinsed
and drained

a large bunch of fresh coriander/cilantro,
finely chopped

sea salt and freshly ground black pepper

SERVES 4–6

Heat the ghee in the base of a tagine or in a heavy-based saucepan, stir in the onion, ginger, garlic and sugar and sauté for 2–3 minutes until they soften and begin to colour. Add the cumin and coriander seeds and cook for a further 1–2 minutes, then stir in the Ras el Hanout and toss in the lentils, making sure they are thoroughly coated.

Pour in enough water to cover the lentils by about 2.5 cm/1 inch and bring it to the boil. Reduce the heat, put on the lid and simmer gently for about 35 minutes, until all the liquid has been absorbed but the lentils still have a bite to them.

Season the lentils with salt and pepper to taste, toss in most of the coriander/cilantro and garnish with the rest.

aubergine and courgette tagine with apricots and dates

This delicious tagine is like a Moroccan 'ratatouille' with the additional burst of sweet and spicy flavours from the dried fruits and the ras el hanout. It is a lovely dish to serve on its own with chunks of fresh crusty bread and a dollop of yogurt, but you can also serve it with couscous.

Heat the oil with the butter in the base of a tagine or in a heavy-based saucepan, stir in the onion and garlic and sauté for 1–2 minutes to soften. Toss in the aubergines/eggplants and courgettes/zucchini and cook for a further 3–4 minutes, then add the pepper, dates, apricots, Ras el Hanout and sugar. Stir in the tomatoes with half the herbs and bring to the boil. Cover with the lid and cook over a medium heat for 30–40 minutes.

Season the tagine with salt and pepper, garnish with the remaining herbs and serve.

3–4 tablespoons olive oil

20 g/1½ tablespoons butter

1 onion, halved lengthways and sliced into half moons

2–3 garlic cloves, chopped

2 aubergines/eggplants, cut into bite-sized chunks

2 courgettes/zucchini, cut into bite-sized chunks

1 red (bell) pepper, halved, deseeded and sliced

150 g/1 cup ready-to-eat stoned/pitted dried dates, halved lengthways

150 g/1 cup ready-to-eat dried apricots, halved

2–3 teaspoons Ras el Hanout (see page 15)

2 teaspoons sugar

2 x 400-g/14-oz. cans chopped tomatoes

a small bunch of fresh flat leaf parsley, finely chopped

a small bunch of fresh coriander/cilantro, finely chopped

sea salt and freshly ground black pepper

SERVES 4–6

carrot and potato tagine with peas

This is a classic peasant or 'poor man's' tagine, which can be easily adapted to suit the season or the budget by substituting the peas with beans, chickpeas, or chopped turnip or cabbage. Serve with plain couscous, rice or chunks of crusty bread.

2-3 tablespoons ghee, smen or argan oil, or 1 tablespoon olive oil plus 1 tablespoon butter

2 onions, halved and sliced with the grain

4 garlic cloves, chopped

25 g/a 1-inch piece of fresh ginger, peeled and chopped

1-2 red chillies, deseeded and finely chopped

1 teaspoon cumin seeds

1 teaspoon coriander seeds

2 teaspoons ground turmeric

8 small potatoes, peeled and left whole

3-4 carrots, peeled and cut into 3-4 chunks

600 ml/2½ cups vegetable stock

225 g/1½ cups freshly shelled or frozen peas

a small bunch of fresh flat leaf parsley, finely chopped

a small bunch of fresh mint, finely chopped

sea salt and freshly ground black pepper

SERVES 4

Heat the ghee in the base of a tagine or in a heavy-based saucepan, stir in the onions, garlic, ginger, chillies and the cumin and coriander seeds and sauté for 2–3 minutes. Add the turmeric and the potatoes and carrots. Pour in the stock and bring it to the boil. Put the lid on the tagine, reduce the heat and cook gently for 15–20 minutes, until the potatoes and carrots are tender.

Toss in the peas, add half the parsley and mint, and season with salt and pepper. Add a little extra water, if necessary, put the lid back on and cook gently for 5–6 minutes. Garnish with the rest of the parsley and mint before serving.

spicy carrot and chickpea tagine with turmeric and coriander

Chickpeas and other pulses often feature in the tagines of arid areas and poorer communities as they provide protein and nourishment where meat is scarce. Combined with vegetables and spices, hearty tagines like this one are also popular in the street stalls and cafés of Fes and Marrakesh.

2 tablespoons ghee or smen, or 1 tablespoon olive oil plus 1 tablespoon butter

1 large onion, finely chopped

1–2 red chillies, deseeded and finely chopped

2–3 garlic cloves, finely chopped

2 teaspoons cumin seeds

2 teaspoons coriander seeds

1–2 teaspoons sugar

2–3 carrots, peeled, halved lengthways and thickly sliced

2 x 400-g/14-oz. cans chickpeas, thoroughly rinsed and drained

2 teaspoons ground turmeric

1 teaspoon ground cinnamon

a bunch of fresh coriander/cilantro leaves, finely chopped

sea salt and freshly ground black pepper

SERVES 4

Heat the ghee in the base of a tagine or in a heavy-based saucepan, stir in the onion, chillies, garlic, cumin and coriander seeds and the sugar and sauté for 2–3 minutes, until the onion begins to colour. Toss in the carrot and cook for a further 1–2 minutes, then add the chickpeas.

Stir in the turmeric and cinnamon and pour in enough water to cover the base of the tagine. Bring the water to the boil, put on the lid, and cook over a gentle heat for 20–25 minutes, topping up the water if necessary, until the carrots are tender.

Season the tagine with salt and pepper, stir in most of the coriander/cilantro, and garnish with the remainder.

tagine of butternut squash, shallots, sultanas and pomegranate syrup

Variations of this sweet and spicy tagine are often served in the restaurants of Tangier, Casablanca, Rabat and Fes, where the influence of the French, the Moors and the Arabs is often evident in the dishes. Enjoy the flavours of this tagine with a lemon or herb couscous and a tangy salad.

2 tablespoons olive or argan oil

4 garlic cloves, peeled and smashed

2 teaspoons fennel seeds

8-12 shallots, peeled and left whole

2-3 tablespoons sultanas/golden raisins

1-2 teaspoons Harissa (see page 12)

1 butternut squash, peeled, deseeded and cut into bite-sized chunks

2 tablespoons honey

2 tablespoons pomegranate syrup

a small bunch of fresh coriander/cilantro leaves, finely chopped

sea salt and freshly ground black pepper

1-2 tablespoons pomegranate seeds, to garnish

SERVES 4

Heat the oil in the base of a tagine or in a heavy-based saucepan, stir in the garlic and fennel seeds and sauté for 1–2 minutes, until fragrant. Add the shallots, rolling them around in the oil, and cook for a further 2 minutes. Toss in the sultanas/golden raisins and cook until they plump up, then stir in the Harissa and the butternut squash.

Pour in enough water to just cover the base of the tagine and bring it to the boil. Put on the lid and cook the tagine over a medium heat for 15 minutes, until the butternut squash is tender. Stir in the honey and pomegranate sryup and cook over a medium heat for a further 10 minutes.

Season the tagine with salt and pepper, stir in most of the coriander/cilantro and garnish with the rest of the coriander/cilantro and the pomegranate seeds.

tagine of roasted potatoes, onions and fennel with sumac and balsamic vinegar

500 g/1 lb. 2 oz. new potatoes, unpeeled

2 tablespoons ghee, smen or argan oil, or 1 tablespoon olive oil plus 1 tablespoon butter

2 onions, halved lengthways and sliced with the grain

2 fennel bulbs, trimmed and finely sliced in their skins

4-6 garlic cloves, smashed in their skins

2-3 tablespoons balsamic vinegar

1-2 teaspoons sumac

a small bunch of fresh flat leaf parsley, roughly chopped

sea salt and freshly ground black pepper

SERVES 4

Potatoes often feature in peasant or 'poor man's' tagines with onions and garlic and perhaps a few herbs or spices. This roasted variation of a classic poor man's tagine is delicious served with a fresh tomato or fruit-based salad.

Preheat oven to 200°C (400°F) Gas 6.

Put the potatoes in a large saucepan and top up with enough water to cover them. Bring the water to the boil and cook the potatoes for 5–6 minutes. Drain, refresh them under cold water, then thickly slice.

Heat the ghee in the base of a tagine or in a heavy-based casserole, stir in the onions and sauté for 3–4 minutes, until they begin to soften and colour. Stir in the fennel and garlic cloves and cook for a further 2–3 minutes. Toss in the potatoes and season with salt and pepper.

Put the tagine in the preheated oven, uncovered, and cook for 35–40 minutes, until the potatoes are golden and slightly roasted.

Toss in the balsamic vinegar and sprinkle the sumac and parsley over the tagine, to serve.

2 tablespoons ghee, smen or argan oil, or 1 tablespoon olive oil plus 1 tablespoon butter

40 g/a 2-inch piece of fresh ginger, peeled and finely chopped

2 cinnamon sticks

8–12 small, round shallots, peeled and left whole

8 garlic cloves, peeled and left whole

1 yam, peeled and cut into bite-sized chunks

300 ml/1¼ cups vegetable stock

8–12 ready-to-eat dried stoned/pitted prunes

2 tablespoons honey

grated zest and freshly squeezed juice of 1 orange

1 tablespoon orange blossom water

a small bunch of fresh mint leaves, finely chopped or shredded

sea salt and freshly ground black pepper

SERVES 4

tagine of yam, shallots, garlic and prunes with orange

This syrupy tagine is delicious served as an accompaniment to other tagines, or on its own with chunks of crusty bread to mop up the sweet sauce. Serve it with a tangy, crunchy or leafy salad to balance the sweetness.

Heat the ghee in the base of a tagine or in a heavy-based saucepan, stir in the ginger and cinnamon sticks and sauté for 1–2 minutes. Toss in the shallots, rolling them over in the ginger and ghee until they begin to colour, then add the garlic cloves and yam and cook for a further 1–2 minutes.

Pour in the vegetable stock, making sure you have enough to cover the base of the tagine, and bring it to the boil. Put on the lid, reduce the heat and cook gently for 15 minutes. Toss in the prunes, honey, orange zest and juice, and the orange blossom water, put the lid back on and cook over a medium heat for a further 10 minutes.

Remove the lid and continue to cook over a medium heat, until the liquid reduces and begins to caramelize. Season the tagine with salt and pepper and stir in most of the mint. Serve the tagine garnished with the remaining mint.

sweet potato tagine with green olives and orange blossom water

Sweet potatoes and yams are popular in village tagines as they work well with spices, dried fruits and tangy flavourings and they tend to fill the stomach quite quickly. This unusual tagine from Casablanca is a more sophisticated version with the floral notes of orange blossom water and can be served hot in the winter, or at room temperature in the summer with wedges of lemon to squeeze over it. A spicy couscous dish makes the perfect accompaniment.

2-3 tablespoons olive or argan oil

1 onion, roughly chopped

1 teaspoon cumin seeds

25 g/a 1-inch piece of fresh ginger, peeled and finely chopped

2-3 sweet potatoes, peeled and cut into bite-sized chunks

½ teaspoon smoked paprika

8-12 cracked green olives, rinsed and drained

1 Preserved Lemon (see page 16), finely chopped

freshly squeezed juice of ½ lemon

3-4 tablespoons orange blossom water

sea salt and freshly ground black pepper

a small bunch of fresh coriander/cilantro, finely chopped, to garnish

SERVES 4–6

Heat the olive oil in the base of a tagine or in a heavy-based saucepan, stir in the onion and sauté for 2–3 minutes, until it begins to soften and colour. Add the cumin seeds and ginger and cook until fragrant. Toss in the sweet potatoes along with the paprika and pour in just enough water to just cover the base of the tagine. Put on the lid and cook gently for 10–15 minutes, until the sweet potato is tender, but firm, and the liquid has reduced.

Toss in the olives, Preserved Lemon, lemon juice and orange blossom water. Replace the lid and cook gently for a further 10 minutes. Season the tagine with salt and pepper to taste, garnish with the coriander/cilantro and serve.

pumpkin, apple and sultana tagine with chermoula

Chermoula is often used as a marinade for fish in tagines and grilled dishes, but it is sometimes employed in vegetable dishes too, particularly in the coastal regions. The combination of pumpkin and apple with the tangy, spicy chermoula makes this an interesting accompaniment to plain grilled or roasted dishes, as well as plain couscous.

2 tablespoons olive or argan oil

700 g/1 lb. 9 oz. pumpkin, skinned, deseeded and cut into bite-sized chunks

2 crisp apples, peeled, cored and cut into segments or bite-sized chunks

2 tablespoons sultanas/golden raisins or raisins

1 teaspoon smoked paprika

1 quantity Chermoula (see page 14)

sea salt and freshly ground black pepper

a small bunch of fresh mint leaves, finely shredded, to garnish

SERVES 4–6

Heat the oil in the base of a tagine or in a heavy-based saucepan, toss in the pumpkin and sauté for 1–2 minutes. Add the apple and sultanas/golden raisins and cook for a further 1–2 minutes, until the sultanas/golden raisins plump up. Sprinkle in the paprika, stir in the Chermoula and pour in enough water to cover the base of the tagine. Bring the water to the boil, put on the lid and cook over a medium heat for 20–25 minutes, until the pumpkin is tender.

Season the tagine with salt and pepper, garnish with a little shredded mint, and serve.

tagine of roasted butternut squash with rosemary, almonds and apricots

This is a tagine for banquets or celebration in the home. When prepared for large numbers, the butternut squash is laid out in baking pans but for a family meal, it can be prepared in the base of a wide tagine. You can serve the roasted squash as an accompaniment to other tagines, or on its own with a spicy couscous.

1 butternut squash

2–3 tablespoons olive, argan or pumpkin seed oil

2 garlic cloves, crushed

4 sprigs of fresh rosemary

2 tablespoons flaked/slivered almonds

1–2 balls of preserved stem ginger, finely chopped

6–8 ready-to-eat dried apricots, finely chopped

1–2 tablespoons honey

sea salt and freshly ground black pepper

SERVES 4

Preheat oven to 200°C (400°F) Gas 6.

Cut the butternut squash in half lengthways and scoop out the seeds with a spoon. Cut the halves in half lenthways again and put them, skin-side down, in the base of a tagine or in a heavy-based casserole. Rub the oil and garlic over the butternut flesh and thread the rosemary sprigs diagonally through the fleshiest part (if the flesh is too firm, push a thin skewer through first to form the opening). Season the squash with salt and pepper and place the tagine in the preheated oven for 30–35 minutes, until the flesh is tender.

Meanwhile, roast the almonds in a dry frying pan until they turn golden brown and emit a nutty aroma. In a small bowl, combine the roasted almonds with the stem ginger and apricots.

Take the tagine out of the oven and spoon some of the almond, ginger and apricot mixture into the hollow of each butternut squash slice, then scatter the rest around the dish. Drizzle the honey over the top and return the tagine to the oven for a further 10 minutes. Serve immediately.

baked vegetable tagine with preserved lemon

Oven-cooked tagines are either roasted in the open tagine base, or they are baked in traditional Berber tagines, which have a flatter domed lid compared with the classic, steep conical one. This oven-baked Berber recipe for seasonal vegetables is a delicious way of celebrating the harvest, served hot with a mound of buttery couscous.

3-4 tablespoons olive or argan oil

2 onions, halved and sliced with the grain

4 garlic cloves, finely chopped

40 g/a 2-inch piece of fresh ginger, peeled and finely chopped

2 red chillies, deseeded and finely chopped

2 teaspoons cumin seeds

2 teaspoons coriander seeds

1-2 teaspoons sugar

4 potatoes, peeled and thickly sliced

2 carrots, peeled and thickly sliced

1 small cabbage, trimmed and cut into thick slices

about 600 ml/2½ cups vegetable stock

225 g/1½ cups freshly shelled or frozen peas

1 Preserved Lemon (see page 16), finely sliced

a bunch of fresh mint, finely shredded

a bunch of fresh coriander/cilantro, finely chopped

6 large tomatoes, finely sliced

1 tablespoon butter, cut into little pieces

sea salt and freshly ground black pepper

SERVES 4–6

Preheat oven to 180°C (350°F) Gas 4.

Heat the oil in the base of a tagine or in a heavy-based saucepan, stir in the onions and sauté for 2 minutes to soften them a little. Stir in the garlic, ginger, chillies, cumin and coriander seeds, and the sugar and cook for a further 1–2 minutes, until the onions begin to colour.

Toss in the potatoes and carrots and cook for 1–2 minutes, then stir in the cabbage. Pour in the stock, making sure it almost covers the vegetables, and bring it to the boil. Put the lid on the tagine and put it in the preheated oven for about 30 minutes.

Add all of the peas and most of the Preserved Lemon, mint and coriander/cilantro to the tagine, and season with salt and pepper. Arrange the tomato slices, overlapping each other, on top of the vegetables and scatter the butter over the tomatoes. Return the tagine, without the lid, to the oven for about 15 minutes more, until the tomatoes are lightly browned.

Garnish the tagine with the rest of the preserved lemon, mint and coriander/cilantro, and serve.

roasted sweet potato tagine with ginger, cinnamon and honey

This is a very tasty way of cooking potatoes, ideal as an accompaniment for numerous grilled and roasted dishes, or simply on its own with garlic-flavoured yogurt and chunks of crusty bread.

2 tablespoons ghee, or 1 tablespoon olive oil plus 1 tablespoon butter

50 g/a 2-inch piece of fresh ginger, peeled and cut into very thin sticks

4 garlic cloves, peeled and cut into thin sticks

4–6 cinnamon sticks

4–6 sweet potatoes, peeled and cut into bite-sized chunks

1–2 tablespoons runny honey

sea salt and freshly ground black pepper

a small bunch of fresh coriander/cilantro, finely chopped, to garnish

FOR THE YOGURT:

400 ml/1⅔ cups thick, creamy yogurt

1–2 garlic cloves, crushed

sea salt and freshly ground black pepper

SERVES 4–6

Preheat oven to 200°C (400°F) Gas 6.

Melt the ghee in the base of a tagine or in a heavy-based casserole, stir in the ginger, garlic and cinnamon sticks and sauté for 1 minute. Add the sweet potatoes and toss in the spices to coat, then pop the tagine, without the lid, in the preheated oven for 45 minutes.

Remove the tagine from the oven and toss the potatoes in the ghee and flavourings, season with salt and pepper and drizzle over the honey. Return the tagine to the oven for a further 10–15 minutes, until the sweet potato is tender and slightly caramelized.

In a small bowl, beat together the yogurt and crushed garlic, then season with salt and pepper.

Garnish the sweet potato with the coriander/cilantro and serve it with the garlic-flavoured yogurt.

COUSCOUS

plain buttery couscous

To many a Moroccan, a mound of light, buttery couscous is perfection on a plate. After all the fluffing and aerating of the couscous, each grain should be separated and the dish should emit the sweet, warming aroma of melted butter. Go further and add almonds and cinnamon to the dish and what you have is, undoubtedly, the king of couscous dishes – the most popular and practical of all.

350 g/2 cups couscous

½ teaspoon sea salt

400 ml/1⅔ cups warm water

2 tablespoons sunflower or olive oil

25 g/2 tablespoons butter, cut into little pieces

FOR THE TOP (OPTIONAL):

15 g/1 tablespoon butter

2–3 tablespoons blanched almonds, halved

1–2 teaspoons ground cinnamon

SERVES 4

Preheat the oven to 180°C (350°F) Gas 4.

Put the couscous in an ovenproof dish. Stir the salt into the warm water and pour it over the couscous. Stir once to make sure all the grains are submerged in the water, cover the dish with a clean tea/dish towel and leave the couscous to absorb the water for 10 minutes.

Rake a fork through the couscous to loosen the grains then, using your fingers, rub the oil into them, lifting the grains up into the air and letting them fall back into the dish to aerate them. Dot the top of the couscous with the butter, cover the dish with a piece of dampened baking paper and pop it into the preheated oven for 15 minutes to heat through.

Meanwhile, prepare the almonds for the top, if using. Melt the butter in a heavy-based pan, stir in the almonds and sauté over a medium heat until they begin to turn golden. Drain on paper towels.

Take the couscous out of the oven and fluff up the grains with a fork, then tip it onto a serving dish, piling it into a pyramid. If using, scatter the almonds over and around the couscous pyramid. Rubbing the cinnamon between your fingers, dust it over the top, or in lines down the sides of the pyramid. Serve immediately.

couscous with turmeric and ginger

You can make this couscous as spicy as you like by adding more chilli or ginger. It goes well with both the sweet and the spicy tagines and it is delicious served on its own with a dollop of thick creamy yogurt and a Moroccan chutney or pickle.

500 g/2¾ cups couscous

1 teaspoon sea salt

600 ml/2½ cups warm water

2 tablespoons ghee or argan oil, or 1 tablespoon olive oil plus 1 tablespoon butter

40 g/a 2-inch piece of fresh ginger, peeled and very finely chopped

1 red chilli, deseeded and finely chopped

2 teaspoons ground turmeric

a small bunch of fresh coriander/cilantro, finely chopped

sea salt and freshly ground black pepper

SERVES 4–6

Tip the couscous into a large bowl. Stir the salt into the hot water and pour it over the couscous. Stir once to make sure all the grains are submerged in the water, cover the bowl with a clean tea/dish towel and leave the couscous to absorb the water for 10 minutes. Rake the couscous with a fork to break up the grains.

Heat the ghee in a heavy-based saucepan, stir in the ginger and chilli and sauté for 2–3 minutes, until they begin to colour. Add the turmeric and couscous and toss everything together, making sure it is thoroughly mixed. Toss in most of the coriander/cilantro and season with salt and pepper.

Tip the couscous into a serving dish, garnish with the rest of the coriander/cilantro and serve.

couscous with braised fennel, courgette and orange

Couscous with cooked vegetables can be served as a side dish or as a dish on its own. Vibrant orange and green, with bursts of citrusy flavour, this couscous dish is a colourful and refreshing accompaniment to tagines and grills.

500 g/2¾ cups couscous

½ teaspoon sea salt

600 ml/2½ cups warm water

4 tablespoons olive oil

50 g/3½ tablespoons butter, cut into little pieces

2 fennel bulbs

1 courgette/zucchini

1-2 teaspoons aniseed seeds

freshly squeezed juice of 2 oranges and grated zest of 1 orange

1 tablespoon honey

1 tablespoon orange blossom water

sea salt and freshly ground black pepper

SERVES 4

Preheat the oven to 180°C (350°F) Gas 4.

Put the couscous in an ovenproof dish. Stir the salt into the warm water and pour it over the couscous. Stir once to make sure all the grains are submerged in the water, cover the dish with a clean tea/dish towel and leave the couscous to absorb the water for 10 minutes.

Rake a fork through the couscous to loosen the grains then, using your fingers, rub 2 tablespoons of the oil into them, lifting the grains up into the air and letting them fall back into the dish to aerate them. Dot the top of the couscous with half of the butter, cover the dish with a piece of dampened baking paper and pop it into the preheated oven for 10–15 minutes to heat through.

Trim the fennel bulbs, remove the outer leaves and quarter them. Trim off the courgette/zucchini ends, cut it in half, then slice it lengthways.

Heat the remaining oil in the base of a tagine or in a heavy-based saucepan, stir in the aniseed and grated orange zest and sauté for 1–2 minutes, until fragrant. Toss in the quartered fennel bulbs, then pour in the orange juice. Put the lid on the tagine and cook gently for 3–4 minutes.

Add the courgette/zucchini to the tagine, along with the remaining butter and toss through. Season with salt and pepper and drizzle the honey over the top. Cover and cook for another 3–4 minutes, until the fennel and courgette/zucchini are tender. Remove the lid and boil any remaining liquid for 3–4 minutes, until it caramelizes a little, then splash the orange blossom water over the vegetables.

Pile the couscous into a mound on a shallow serving dish and spoon the fennel and courgette/zucchini over and around it. Drizzle the caramelized juice over the top and serve.

couscous with seven vegetables

This is a classic couscous dish, which is enjoyed throughout the Maghreb, varying from region to region and dictated by the season. The number seven is believed to bring good luck so, as long as you have that number of vegetables in the accompanying stew, you can be flexible with the variety. If you have a couscoussier, you can steam the couscous in the compartment above the vegetables cooking in the stock in the lower part.

FOR THE COUSCOUS:

500 g/2¾ cups couscous

1 teaspoon sea salt

600 ml/2½ cups warm water

2 tablespoons sunflower oil

25 g/2 tablespoons butter, cut into little pieces

FOR THE VEGETABLE STEW:

1.5 litres/6 cups vegetable stock

6 garlic cloves, peeled and smashed

2 bay leaves

a few bushy sprigs of fresh rosemary

6-8 peppercorns

2 onions, peeled and cut into quarters

2 carrots, peeled, halved lengthways and cut into long, thick strips

2 sweet potatoes, peeled, halved lengthways and cut into long, thick strips

1 small marrow, deseeded, halved and cut into long, thick strips

3 celery stalks, trimmed and cut into 3 pieces

2-3 leeks, trimmed and cut into 3-4 pieces

2-3 tomatoes, cut into quarters

2 teaspoons honey

1 generous tablespoon Harissa (see page 12)

sea salt and freshly ground black pepper

SERVES 6

Preheat the oven to 180°C (350°F) Gas 4.

Put the couscous in an ovenproof dish. Stir the salt into the warm water and pour it over the couscous. Stir once to make sure all the grains are submerged in the water, cover the dish with a clean tea/dish towel and leave the couscous to absorb the water for 10 minutes.

Meanwhile, put the stock in a large saucepan and bring it to the boil. Stir in the garlic, bay leaves, rosemary, peppercorns and 1 teaspoon salt. Add the onions, carrots, sweet potatoes and marrow and cook for 5 minutes, then add the celery and leeks. Cover the saucepan and cook gently for 20–25 minutes. Check the seasoning, then stir in the tomatoes, honey and 1 teaspoon of the Harissa.

Rake a fork through the couscous to loosen the grains then, using your fingers, rub the oil into them, lifting the grains up into the air and letting them fall back into the dish to aerate them. Dot the top of the couscous with the butter, cover the dish with a piece of dampened baking paper and pop it into the preheated oven for 15 minutes to heat through.

Pile the couscous into a mound on a shallow serving dish. Using a slotted spoon, lift the vegetables out of the stock and place them around the couscous. Pour the stock into a bowl or jug/pitcher, spoon the rest of the Harissa into a small bowl and serve both with the vegetables and couscous.

couscous with dried fruit and nuts

This impressive-looking couscous dish is delicious served as a course on its own. You can vary the dried ingredients, but make sure the couscous grains are packed with lots of nutty and fruity goodness. Serve it as a meal on its own with yogurt or as an accompaniment to grills and roasts.

500 g/2¾ cups couscous

1 teaspoon sea salt

a pinch of saffron threads

600 ml/2½ cups warm water

3 tablespoons sunflower oil

2 tablespoons ghee or smen, or 1 tablespoon olive oil plus 1 tablespoon butter

2 tablespoons blanched almonds, cut into slivers

1 tablespoon shelled pistachio nuts

1 tablespoon pine nuts

120 g/scant 1 cup ready-to-eat dried apricots, cut into slivers

120 g/scant 1 cup dried dates, chopped

2 tablespoons (zante) currants or raisins

2 teaspoons ground cinnamon

3 tablespoons icing/confectioners' sugar

SERVES 4–6

Preheat the oven to 180°C (350°F) Gas 4.

Put the couscous in an ovenproof dish. Stir the salt and saffron into the warm water and pour it over the couscous. Stir once to make sure all the grains are submerged in the water, cover the dish with a clean tea/dish towel and leave the couscous to absorb the water for 10 minutes.

Rake a fork through the couscous to loosen the grains then, using your fingers, rub the oil into them, lifting the grains up into the air and letting them fall back into the dish to aerate them.

Heat the ghee in a heavy-based saucepan, stir in most of the almond slivers and sauté for 1–2 minutes. Toss in the pistachios, pine nuts and dried fruit and cook for a further 1–2 minutes, then pour the mixture into the dish with the couscous and toss through. Cover the dish with a piece of dampened baking paper and pop it into the preheated oven for 15 minutes to heat through.

Pile the couscous into a mound on a large, shallow serving dish and sprinkle with the cinnamon and sugar – this is usually done in alternate stripes up and down the mound. Toast the reserved almond slivers and scatter them over the top, to serve.

couscous tfaia

A traditional 'tfaia' embodies several features – onions, saffron and sultanas or raisins. Other ingredients can be added but this is tfaia at its simplest. It livens up a simple dish of couscous and can be served with most tagines.

FOR THE COUSCOUS:

350 g/2 cups couscous

1 teaspoon sea salt

400 ml/1⅔ cups warm water

25 g/2 tablespoons butter, cut into little pieces

FOR THE TFAIA:

2-3 tablespoons ghee or smen, or 1 tablespoon olive oil plus 1 tablespoon butter

4 onions, finely sliced

50 g/a 2-inch piece of fresh ginger, peeled and chopped

4 cinnamon sticks

2 tablespoons sultanas/golden raisins

1 teaspoon saffron threads, soaked in 4 tablespoons water

2 tablespoons honey

sea salt and freshly ground black pepper

a bunch of fresh coriander/cilantro, finely chopped, to garnish

SERVES 4

Preheat the oven to 180°C (350°F) Gas 4.

Put the couscous in an ovenproof dish. Stir the salt into the warm water and pour it over the couscous. Stir once to make sure all the grains are submerged in the water, cover the dish with a clean tea/dish towel and leave the couscous to absorb the water for 10 minutes.

Rake a fork through the couscous to loosen the grains then, using your fingers, rub the oil into them, lifting the grains up into the air and letting them fall back into the dish to aerate them. Dot the top of the couscous with the butter, cover the dish with a piece of dampened baking paper and pop it into the preheated oven for 15 minutes to heat through.

Meanwhile, heat the ghee in the base of a tagine or in a heavy-based saucepan, stir in the onions and ginger and cinnamon sticks and sauté for 2–3 minutes. Add the sultanas/golden raisins and saffron, with its soaking water, cover the pan and cook gently for 8–10 minutes. Season with salt and pepper, stir in the honey and cook the tfaia gently for about 5 minutes.

Pile the couscous into a mound on a shallow serving dish, hollow out the top and spoon the tfaia into it. Garnish with the coriander/cilantro and serve.

lemon couscous with roasted vegetables and lime

For this recipe, you can roast the vegetables in the oven or cut them into bite-sized chunks, thread them onto skewers, and grill them over a barbecue. Generally, peppers, aubergines/eggplants, courgettes/zucchini, shallots and cherry tomatoes are used for roasting and grilling, but you can vary the mix with other seasonal vegetables. Serve with a dollop of yogurt or a drizzle of buttermilk, and a chutney, relish, or a crunchy salad.

FOR THE ROASTED VEGETABLES:

8 baby aubergines/eggplants, cut in half lengthways, keeping the stalk intact

2 courgettes/zucchini, halved and cut into quarters lengthways

2 (bell) peppers, deseeded and cut into quarters lengthways

4 garlic cloves, cut into 4 lengthways

40 g/a 2-inch piece of fresh ginger, peeled and cut into thin sticks

1-2 teaspoons sugar or honey

1-2 teaspoons finely chopped dried chilli

100 ml/6 tablespoons olive oil

sea salt

FOR THE COUSCOUS:

500 g/2¾ cups couscous

½ teaspoon sea salt

600 ml/2½ cups warm water

1-2 tablespoons olive oil

1 Preserved Lemon (see page 16), finely chopped

1 tablespoon butter, cut into little pieces

2 limes, cut into quarters

SERVES 4–6

Preheat the oven to 200°C (400°F) Gas 6.

Put all the vegetables in an ovenproof dish with the garlic and ginger. Add the sugar and chilli and toss everything together well. Pour over the oil, sprinkle with salt and put the vegetables in the preheated oven for about 50 minutes, turning them from time to time, until they are tender and nicely browned.

Meanwhile, put the couscous in an ovenproof dish. Stir the salt into the warm water and pour it over the couscous. Stir once to make sure all the grains are submerged in the water, cover the dish with a clean tea/dish towel and leave the couscous to absorb the water for 10 minutes.

Rake a fork through the couscous to loosen the grains then, using your fingers, rub the oil into them, lifting the grains up into the air and letting them fall back into the dish to aerate them. Toss in the Preserved Lemon and dot the top of the couscous with the butter, cover the dish with a piece of dampened baking paper and pop it into the preheated oven for 15 minutes to heat through.

To serve, tip the couscous onto a plate in a mound. Make a dip in the top and arrange the vegetables over and around the couscous. Spoon some of the roasting oil over the top of the mound and arrange the lime wedges around the edge to squeeze over the vegetables.

saffron couscous with roasted coconut and pistachios

This simple couscous dish is light and fragrant and often served on its own between courses to stabilize the palate after spicy dishes. It can also be served alongside salads and dips as a starter, or as an accompaniment to grilled and roasted vegetable dishes.

350 g/2 cups couscous

½ teaspoon sea salt

a pinch of saffron threads

400 ml/1⅔ cups warm water

3 tablespoons desiccated/dried shredded coconut

2 tablespoons olive oil

25 g/2 tablespoons butter, cut into little pieces

1–2 tablespoons finely ground pistachio nuts

freshly ground black pepper

SERVES 4

Preheat the oven to 180°C (350°F) Gas 4.

Put the couscous into an ovenproof dish. Stir the salt and saffron into the warm water and leave to stand for 5 minutes so that the threads impart their yellow dye. Pour the saffron water over the couscous. Stir once to make sure all the grains are submerged in the water and the saffron threads are dispersed. Cover the dish with a clean tea/dish towel and leave the couscous to absorb the water for 10 minutes.

Meanwhile, roast the coconut in a small heavy-based frying pan until it begins to turn golden and emits a nutty aroma.

Rake a fork through the couscous to loosen the grains then, using your fingers, rub the oil into them, lifting the grains up into the air and letting them fall back into the dish to aerate them. Toss in the roasted coconut and season with pepper. Dot the top of the couscous with the butter, cover the dish with a piece of dampened baking paper and pop it into the preheated oven for 15 minutes to heat through.

Pile the couscous into a mound on a shallow serving dish and scatter the ground pistachio nuts over it, or in lines up and down the mound, and serve.

couscous with hot apricot chutney and halloumi

2-3 tablespoons sunflower oil

225 g/8 oz. halloumi, cut into thin slices

a small bunch of fresh coriander/cilantro, finely chopped, to garnish

FOR THE CHUTNEY:

225 g/1½ cups ready-to-eat dried apricots, finely chopped

1 tart green apple, peeled, cored and finely chopped

1 onion, finely chopped

2-3 garlic cloves, finely chopped

1 tablespoon peeled and grated fresh ginger

1 tablespoon sultanas/golden raisins

2 cinnamon sticks

freshly squeezed juice and grated zest of 1 lemon

150 ml/⅔ cup white wine vinegar

a pinch of chilli powder

120 g/½ cup plus 1 tablespoon granulated sugar

1 tablespoon honey

2-3 tablespoons orange blossom water

FOR THE COUSCOUS:

350 g/2 cups couscous

1 teaspoon sea salt

400 ml/1⅔ cups warm water

25 g/2 tablespoons butter, cut into little pieces

SERVES 4

Held as it is in such high esteem, couscous is often served as a course on its own or, as in this case, as a rather special snack. This is also a good way of using up leftover couscous by livening it up with a spicy chutney.

Preheat the oven to 180°C (350°F) Gas 4.

Put all the chutney ingredients, except the honey and orange blossom water, into the base of a tagine or in a heavy-based saucepan and bring the liquid to the boil, stirring all the time. Cover with the lid and cook gently for 15–20 minutes, stirring from time to time, until the mixture is thick, adding a little water if necessary.

Meanwhile, put the couscous in an ovenproof dish. Stir the salt into the warm water and pour it over the couscous. Stir once to make sure all the grains are submerged in the water, cover the dish with a clean tea/dish towel and leave the couscous to absorb the water for 10 minutes.

Rake a fork through the couscous to loosen the grains then, using your fingers, rub the oil into them, lifting the grains up into the air and letting them fall back into the dish to aerate them. Dot the top of the couscous with the butter, cover the dish with a piece of dampened baking paper and pop it into the preheated oven for 15 minutes to heat through.

Stir the honey and orange blossom water into the chutney mixture and cook gently for a further 5–10 minutes, until the mixture is thick and fragrant, then season with salt.

Heat the sunflower oil in a heavy-based frying pan and fry the halloumi for 3–4 minutes each side, until golden brown, then drain on paper towels.

Tip the couscous into a mound on a shallow serving dish, hollow out the top and spoon the chutney into the hollow. Arrange the halloumi slices over the mound. Garnish with the coriander/cilantro and serve immediately.

harissa couscous with pine nuts and fried eggs

This is a tasty street dish, which is also popular in working men's cafés in the markets and ports. It is great served for brunch or for a quick spicy snack late at night. If you want to create a meal around it, replace the eggs with one of the egg tagines, or serve it with pickled chillies and a yogurt-based salad.

350 g/2 cups couscous

1 teaspoon sea salt

400 ml/1⅔ cups warm water

1–2 tablespoons pine nuts

2 tablespoons ghee, or 1 tablespoon olive oil plus 1 tablespoon butter

2 generous teaspoons Harissa (see page 12)

a small bunch of fresh flat leaf parsley, finely chopped

4 eggs

sea salt and freshly ground black pepper

SERVES 4

Put the couscous into a large bowl. Stir the salt into the warm water and pour it over the couscous. Stir once to make sure all the grains are submerged in the water, cover the bowl with a clean tea/dish towel and leave the couscous to absorb the water for 10 minutes. Rake the couscous with a fork to break up the grains.

Dry roast the pine nuts in a heavy-based saucepan, or the base of a tagine, until they begin to turn golden brown. Stir in half of the ghee until it melts, then add the Harissa. Tip the couscous into the pan and toss it in the ghee and Harissa, until it is thoroughly mixed.

Season the couscous, toss in half of the parsley, cover the pan and keep warm.

Heat the remaining ghee in a frying pan and crack the eggs into it. Cover the pan and fry the eggs until the whites are just firm.

Tip the couscous onto a serving dish, place the eggs on top of it, and garnish with the rest of the parsley, to serve.

green couscous with a spring broth, feta and mint

Ideal for a summer lunch as a meal on its own, this couscous dish can be prepared with any young green vegetables in season, such as broad/fava beans, artichokes, broccoli, peas, cabbage, asparagus, baby courgettes/zucchini and spring onions/scallions.

FOR THE COUSCOUS:

500 g/2¾ cups couscous

½ teaspoon sea salt

600 ml/2½ cups warm water

1–2 tablespoons olive oil

a small bunch of fresh flat leaf parsley, finely chopped

a small bunch of fresh dill fronds, finely chopped

a big bunch of fresh mint leaves, finely chopped

1 tablespoon butter

FOR THE BROTH:

1 litre/4 cups vegetable stock

250 g/9 oz. broccoli, trimmed and cut into bite-sized pieces, keeping the small heads intact

1 courgette/zucchini, cut into bite-sized chunks

1 green (bell) pepper, deseeded and cut into bite-sized chunks

250 g/2 cups freshly shelled broad/fava beans

6–8 spring onions/scallions, trimmed and thickly sliced

250 g/2 cups freshly shelled peas

150 g/5½ oz. feta cheese, crumbled

paprika, for dusting

sea salt and freshly ground black pepper

SERVES 4–6

Preheat the oven to 200°C (400°F) Gas 6.

Put the couscous in an ovenproof dish. Stir the salt into the warm water and pour it over the couscous. Stir once to make sure all the grains are submerged in the water, cover the dish with a clean tea/dish towel and leave the couscous to absorb the water for 10 minutes.

Rake a fork through the couscous to loosen the grains then, using your fingers, rub the oil into them, lifting the grains up into the air and letting them fall back into the dish to aerate them. Toss in the chopped herbs, reserving a little chopped mint to garnish, and dot the top of the couscous with the butter. Cover the dish with a piece of dampened baking paper and pop it into the preheated oven for 15 minutes to heat through.

Meanwhile, prepare the vegetable broth. Pour the stock into a heavy-based saucepan and bring it to the boil. Drop in the broccoli, courgette/zucchini, pepper and broad/fava beans and cook over a medium heat for 3–4 minutes. Add the spring onions/scallions and peas and cook for a further 2–3 minutes, until the vegetables are tender but still have a slight bite to them. Season the broth with salt and pepper.

Remove the couscous from the oven, pile it into a mound on a serving plate and make a hollow in the top. Using a slotted spoon, lift the vegetables out of the broth and arrange them in the hollow and around the base of the mound. Moisten the couscous with a little of the broth, scatter the crumbled feta and reserved fresh mint over the top and dust with a little paprika. Pour the rest of the broth into a bowl to pass around for spooning over the couscous.

lemon and orange couscous with walnuts and pomegranate seeds

Light with a citrus burst, this is a delightful couscous dish to serve with the sweet, honey-based tagines. You can also serve it cold by transforming it into a salad with the addition of finely chopped herbs and a light ginger dressing.

Preheat the oven to 180°C (350°F) Gas 4.

Put the couscous in an ovenproof dish. Stir the salt into the warm water and pour it over the couscous. Stir once to make sure all the grains are submerged in the water, cover the dish with a clean tea/dish towel and leave the couscous to absorb the water for 10 minutes.

Meanwhile, use a sharp knife to remove the peel and pith of 1 orange. Cut between the membranes to release the segments, then cut each segment in half and put them aside. Grate the zest of the other orange, then squeeze it to extract the juice. Combine the lemon and orange zest in a bowl and combine the lemon and orange juice in a separate bowl.

Rake a fork through the couscous to loosen the grains then, using your fingers, rub the oil into them, lifting the grains up into the air and letting them fall back into the dish to aerate them. Rub the orange and lemon zest into the grains, cover the couscous dish with a piece of dampened baking paper and pop it into the preheated oven for 10 minutes to heat through.

Remove the dish from the oven and toss in the orange and lemon juice, orange segments (reserve a few for garnishing), walnuts and half the pomegranate seeds. Season the couscous with salt and pepper, cover with the baking paper and return the dish to the oven for another 10 minutes.

Pile the couscous into a mound on a shallow serving dish. Scatter the parsley over the top and garnish with the reserved orange segments and pomegranate seeds. Serve immediately.

500 g/2¾ cups couscous

½ teaspoon sea salt

600 ml/2½ cups warm water

2 oranges

grated zest and freshly squeezed juice of 1 lemon

1–2 tablespoons olive oil

120 g/4 oz. toasted walnuts, roughly chopped

seeds of 1 pomegranate

sea salt and freshly ground black pepper

a small bunch of fresh flat leaf parsley, roughly chopped, to garnish

SERVES 4–6

SALADS,
PICKLES &
PRESERVES

parsley, walnut and tomato salad with pomegranate syrup

Parsley, or mixed herb, salads are quite common accompaniments to tagines as they cut the spice and refresh the palate. The only dressing employed in this salad is the thick, treacle-coloured pomegranate syrup made from sour pomegranates and available in Asian and North African stores. As a substitute, you could use the juice of half a lemon combined with one tablespoon of fortified balsamic vinegar. Serve with toasted flatbreads or to accompany a dip.

a large bunch of fresh flat leaf parsley

2–3 tablespoons shelled walnuts

2–3 tomatoes

1–2 green chillies, deseeded and finely chopped

1 red onion, finely chopped

2 tablespoons pomegranate syrup

sea salt

SERVES 4

Chop the parsley leaves and stalks – not too fine, not too coarse – and tip them into a shallow serving bowl. Chop the walnuts – again not too fine, so that they have a bite to them – and add them to the serving bowl.

Scald the tomatoes in a pan of boiling water for 2–3 seconds, drain and refresh under running cold water to loosen the skins. Peel and quarter the tomatoes, scoop out and discard the seeds and chop them coarsely. Add the tomatoes to the bowl along with the chillies and scatter the onion over the top.

Drizzle the pomegranate syrup over the salad and season well with salt. Leave the salad to sit for 15–20 minutes to allow the onion juice to weep into the salad. Gently toss the salad and serve.

orange and date salad with chillies and preserved lemon

A delight to the eyes and the palate, this is a delicious salad to serve with any type of dish, particularly other spicy dishes. The four ingredients encompass the four pillars of Moroccan culinary tradition – sweet, salty, hot and fruity.

3–4 ripe, sweet oranges

150 g/1 cup moist, dried dates

2–3 tablespoons orange blossom water

½ Preserved Lemon (see page 16)

1 red chilli, deseeded and finely chopped

SERVES 4

Peel the oranges, removing as much of the pith as possible. Place the oranges on a plate to catch the juice and finely slice them into circles or half moons. Remove and discard the seeds, then put them in a shallow bowl.

Slice the dates finely lengthways and scatter them over the oranges. Pour the orange blossom water over the oranges and dates, cover the bowl and leave for 15 minutes so that the flavours mingle and the dates soften.

Cut the Preserved Lemon in half, remove all the flesh, seeds and pith and finely slice or chop the peel. Scatter the Preserved Lemon and chilli over the oranges and dates and gently toss to mix up the flavours a little before serving.

tomato salad with green chilli and coriander

This refreshing salad with tangy lemon and a chilli kick makes an ideal accompaniment to almost any starter, tagine or couscous dish.

4–6 large tomatoes, finely sliced

2 green chillies, deseeded and finely sliced

½ Preserved Lemon (see page 16), finely sliced

1–2 tablespoons olive or argan oil

a small bunch of fresh coriander/cilantro, finely chopped

SERVES 4

Arrange the tomatoes in a shallow serving bowl and scatter the chillies and Preserved Lemon over them. Drizzle the oil over the top and sprinkle with the coriander/cilantro.

dried apricot and apple salad with yogurt and mint

This yogurt-based salad works well as a starter, or as a refreshing accompaniment to spicy tagines and couscous. For a typical home-cooked meal, you could serve this with a fiery bean or lentil tagine, along with a Moroccan chutney or pickled chillies.

1 crisp green apple

freshly squeezed juice of 1 lemon

6–8 tablespoons thick, creamy yogurt

2 garlic cloves, crushed

a small bunch of fresh mint leaves, finely shredded

150 g/1 cup ready-to-eat dried apricots, cut into thin strips

sea salt and freshly ground black pepper

SERVES 4

Peel and core the apple, then finely slice it into matchsticks. Toss them in the lemon juice to prevent them from discolouring.

In a bowl, beat together the yogurt and the garlic. Add most of the mint and season to taste with salt and pepper.

Fold the apricots and apple, along with the lemon juice, into the yogurt, garnish with the rest of the mint and serve.

broad bean and carrot salad with preserved lemon

This is an attractive, fresh-tasting salad for spring or early summer when the broad/fava beans are young and tender. Simple and tangy, it works well as an accompaniment to a variety of starters, or to one of the dried fruit or honey-based tagines.

450 g/3 cups shelled broad/fava beans

2–3 carrots, peeled and finely sliced

1 red onion, sliced

1 preserved lemon, finely sliced

a small bunch of fresh flat leaf parsley, finely chopped

2 tablespoons olive or argan oil

freshly squeezed juice of 1 lemon

2 garlic cloves, crushed

1 teaspoon cumin seeds, crushed

sea salt and freshly ground black pepper

SERVES 4

Bring a pan of water to the boil, add the broad/fava beans and cook for 3–4 minutes. Drain, refresh under cold water and pop any larger beans out of their tough skins.

Put the beans into a salad bowl with the carrots and onion and add the preserved lemon and parsley.

In a small bowl, combine the oil with the lemon juice, garlic and cumin seeds. Season well with salt and pepper and pour it over the salad. Toss thoroughly so everything is well mixed and serve.

grapefruit and pomegranate salad with rosewater

Deliciously refreshing on a hot day and a tremendous palate soother after a hot and spicy tagine or couscous dish, this salad is full of texture – juicy and crunchy – and pretty to look at, too.

2 pink or ruby grapefruit

1 white grapefruit

2 ripe pomegranates

2 tablespoons rosewater

sea salt

1 tablespoon finely shredded fresh mint leaves, to garnish

SERVES 4

Using a small sharp knife, remove the skins and pith from the grapefruit, then carefully cut down in between the membranes to release the fruit segments – catch the juice in a bowl below to add to the salad. Arrange the grapefruit segments in a shallow serving bowl and splash the juice over them.

Cut the pomegranates into quarters, bend each one backwards and scoop out the seeds, removing the pith – again, do this over a bowl to catch the juice. Scatter the seeds and juice over the grapefruit in the serving bowl.

Splash the rosewater over the salad, sprinkle with a little salt and garnish with the mint leaves. Serve chilled, or at room temperature.

tomato jam with cinnamon and roasted sesame seeds

Preserves of this nature are prepared to enjoy as a snack with flatbreads, or to serve as an accompaniment to couscous and grilled dishes. Once prepared, this traditional preserve can be stored in a sealed sterilized jar for several weeks in a cool place.

350 g/12 oz. cherry tomatoes

2-3 tablespoons olive oil

1-2 teaspoons sugar

1 tablespoon tomato purée/paste

2 tablespoons honey

2 teaspoons ground cinnamon

1 tablespoon sesame seeds

sea salt and freshly ground black pepper

SERVES 4

Preheat oven to 200°C (400°F) Gas 6.

Put the tomatoes in an ovenproof dish, pour the olive oil over them, sprinkle with the sugar and put them in the preheated oven to roast for 25–30 minutes, until the skins split and brown a little.

Lift the tomatoes out of the dish, leaving the oil behind, and put them on a chopping board. Leave them to a cool a little, then peel off the skins and chop them to a pulp.

Tip the pulped tomatoes into a heavy-based saucepan with the tomato purée/paste and the roasting oil and bring the mixture to a boil over a medium heat. Stir in the honey and cinnamon, reduce the heat and cook for a further 5–10 minutes, until it is thick.

Meanwhile, dry roast the sesame seeds in a frying pan, until they darken and emit a nutty aroma.

Season the tomato jam with salt and pepper, tip it into a serving bowl and sprinkle the roasted sesame seeds over the top. Serve warm, or at room temperature.

The jam will keep in a sealed, sterilized jar for 2–3 weeks.

lemon, coriander and mint jam

Fresh and tangy, this Moroccan jam is delicious served with sweet or spicy tagines. Sometimes, it is even served on its own to refresh the palate before the next course. You can prepare the jam ahead of time and store it in a sterilized, sealed jar in a cool place for several weeks.

4 lemons

1 tablespoon finely chopped fresh ginger

2 teaspoons coriander seeds

1 teaspoon finely chopped dried red chilli

75 ml/⅓ cup cider or white wine vinegar

3 tablespoons granulated sugar

1 tablespoon finely chopped fresh coriander/cilantro

1 tablespoon finely chopped fresh mint

sea salt

SERVES 4

Using a small sharp knife, carefully peel the skin off 2 of the lemons and remove any pith. Finely shred the skin and put it into a small heavy-based saucepan.

Squeeze all 4 lemons and add the juice to the saucepan along with the ginger, coriander seeds and dried chilli. Pour in the vinegar and sugar and set the pan over a medium heat, stirring all the time, until the sugar has dissolved. Bring the liquid to the boil, then reduce the heat and simmer for 15–20 minutes, until the mixture is almost dry – keep a careful eye on it, stirring from time to time, so that the sugar doesn't burn.

Season the jam with a little salt and leave it to cool in the pan. Toss in the coriander/cilantro and mint and spoon it into a serving bowl to serve as a condiment or palate cleanser.

The jam will keep in a sealed, sterilized jar for 2–3 weeks.

pickled pears with saffron and cinnamon

In the fertile regions of Morocco, where fruit harvests are abundant, the preserving of fruit in jams, relishes, syrups, conserves and pickles is a traditional seasonal activity. Pickled fruit, like these pears, are often devoured with bread and crumbled cheese, or with grilled dishes and sweet tagines.

400 ml/1⅔ cups white wine or cider vinegar

175 g/⅔ cup honey

a pinch of saffron threads

2 cinnamon sticks

4 firm, medium-sized pears, or 8 firm, small pears

a large sterilized jar (see page 4)

MAKES A LARGE JAR

Pour the vinegar and 125 ml/½ cup water into a heavy-based saucepan and add the honey, saffron and cinnamon sticks. Bring the liquid to the boil, stirring all the time, until the honey has dissolved.

Peel the pears. If they are medium-sized, cut them in half lengthways, keeping the stalk intact, deseed and slip them into the pan. If they are small, add them to the pan whole. Reduce the heat and poach the pears gently for 15–20 minutes, until they are tender but still firm.

Lift the pears out of the pickling liquid and arrange them in the sterilized jar. Pour the hot liquid over them and leave to cool. Seal the jar and store the pears in a cool place for 2–3 weeks before serving.

date relish

This moist, sweet and sour relish is often served as a snack or starter with flatbreads and dips or crumbled cheese, but it is also a delicious accompaniment to tangy tagines, or steamed and roasted couscous dishes.

2 tablespoons ghee or argan oil, or 1 tablespoon olive oil plus 1 tablespoon butter

1 red onion, finely chopped

2 garlic cloves, finely chopped

1 teaspoon cumin seeds

150 g/1 cup ready-to-eat dried, stoned/pitted dates, finely chopped

1 pickled or fresh red chilli, finely chopped

2 tablespoons white wine vinegar

2 teaspoons muscovado or soft brown sugar

2 tablespoons date syrup

sea salt

a small sterilized jar (see page 4)

MAKES A SMALL JAR

Heat the ghee in a heavy-based saucepan, stir in the onion, garlic and cumin seeds and sauté until the onion begins to colour.

Toss in the dates and pickled chilli and stir in the vinegar, sugar and date syrup. Cook the relish over a gentle heat for 4–5 minutes, season with salt and leave it to cool in the pan.

Serve the relish as an accompaniment to grilled dishes, tagines or couscous.

The jam will keep in a sealed, sterilized jar for 2–3 weeks.

pickled red chillies

Pickles are often served as appetizers or snacks as they can be refreshing in the heat of the day. However, sliced pickled chillies are often favoured as a garnish for salads and simple couscous dishes to provide a small burst of heat.

400 ml/1⅔ cups white wine or cider vinegar

2 tablespoons sugar

2 teaspoons sea salt

2 teaspoons coriander seeds

8 Serrano or Guajillo chillies

a small sterilized jar (see page 4)

MAKES A SMALL JAR

Pour the vinegar into a saucepan and add the sugar, salt and coriander seeds. Bring the vinegar to the boil, stirring until the sugar has dissolved, then turn off the heat.

Using a small sharp knife, slit each chilli down one side, from the stalk to the tip, making sure you don't cut right through it. Pack the chillies into the jar and pour the vinegar over them, making sure they are completely submerged in the liquid. Seal the jar and keep refrigerated for at least 2 weeks before serving whole as an appetizer, or finely sliced as a topping for salads, tagines and couscous.

pickled purple turnips

Tinged a pretty shade of purple, these pickles are delicious finely sliced and served as appetizers, or in crunchy raw salads.

8 small white turnips

4 garlic cloves, peeled

1 small raw beet(root)

300 ml/1¼ cups white wine vinegar

1 teaspoon sea salt

a large sterilized jar (see page 4)

MAKES A LARGE JAR

Trim and peel the turnips. Rinse them, then pat dry and pop them into the sterilized jar with the garlic.

Trim and peel the beet(root), cut it into 2–3 slices and add them to the jar. Mix together the vinegar, 300 ml/1¼ cups water and the salt and pour the liquid over the turnips and beet(root). Seal the jar with a vinegar-proof lid and store for 1–2 weeks, until the turnips have taken on a purplish-pink hue.

index

figs: tagine of roasted pear with figs, walnuts and cardamom 67

filo (phyllo) pastry: filo fingers stuffed with feta, olives and preserved lemon 26

G

garlic: chermoula 14

chilled almond and garlic soup 38

grapefruit and pomegranate salad with rosewater 134

green couscous with a spring broth, feta and mint 123

H

haricot (navy) beans: bean tagine with harissa and coriander 76

harissa 12

bean tagine with harissa and coriander 76

cauliflower and chickpea tagine with harissa and preserved lemon 75

cracked green olives with cardamom and harissa 23

harissa couscous with pine nuts and fried eggs 120

smoked aubergine and yogurt dip with harissa 29

L

lemon: lemon and orange couscous with walnuts and pomegranate seeds 124

lemon, coriander and mint jam 137

lemons, preserved 16

baked vegetable tagine with preserved lemon 98

broad bean and carrot salad with preserved lemon 133

filo fingers stuffed with feta, olives and preserved lemon 26

lemon couscous with roasted vegetables and lime 115

orange and date salad with chillies and preserved lemon 130

roasted cherry tomato tagine with feta and

preserved lemon 43

lentil tagine with ginger and ras el hanout 79

M

mint: lemon, coriander and mint jam 137

mint tea 18–19

N

navy beans see haricot beans

nuts, couscous with dried fruit and 111

O

okra and tomato tagine with lemon 54

olives: cracked green olives with cardamom and harissa 23

filo fingers stuffed with feta, olives and preserved lemon 26

onion, olive and egg tagine with zahtar 48

sweet potato tagine with green olives and orange blossom water 92

tagine of butter beans, cherry tomatoes and black olives 68

onions: couscous tfaia 112

onion, olive and egg tagine with zahtar 48

tagine of roasted potatoes, onions, and fennel with sumac and balsamic vinegar 88

oranges: couscous with braised fennel, courgette and orange 106–7

lemon and orange couscous with walnuts and pomegranate seeds 124

orange and date salad with chillies and preserved lemon 130

tagine of yam, shallots, garlic and prunes with orange 91

P

parsley, walnut and tomato salad with pomegranate syrup 129

pastries: filo fingers stuffed with feta, olives and preserved lemon 26

pears: pickled pears with saffron and cinnamon 138

tagine of roasted pear with figs, walnuts and cardamom 67

peas, carrot and potato tagine with 82–3

peppers (bell): three pepper tagine with eggs and ras el hanout 57

phyllo pastry see filo pastry

pickles: pickled pears with saffron and cinnamon 138

pickled purple turnips 141

pickled red chillies 141

pine nuts: harissa couscous with pine nuts and fried eggs 120

pistachios, saffron couscous with roasted coconut and 116

plantains: deep-fried plantains with zahtar 25

pomegranate: grapefruit and pomegranate salad with rosewater 134

lemon and orange couscous with walnuts and pomegranate seeds 124

pomegranate syrup, parsley, walnut and tomato salad with 129

potatoes: carrot and potato tagine with peas 82–3

tagine of roasted potatoes, onions, and fennel with sumac and balsamic vinegar 88

preserves: lemon, coriander and mint jam 137

tomato jam with cinnamon and roasted sesame seeds 136

prunes: stuffed prune tagine with walnuts and rosewater 64

tagine of yam, shallots, garlic and prunes with orange 91

pumpkin: creamy pumpkin soup with ginger and chilli honey 34

pumpkin, apple and sultana tagine with chermoula 94

tagine of spicy pumpkin wedges with lime 47

R

ras el hanout 15

chunky tomato soup with vermicelli and ras el hanout 32

lentil tagine with ginger and ras el hanout 79

three pepper tagine with

eggs and ras el hanout 57

relish, date 138

rose petals, strained yogurt and cucumber dip with 30–1

rosewater: grapefruit and pomegranate salad with rosewater 134

stuffed prune tagine with walnuts and rosewater 64

runner bean tagine with tomato and dill 58

S

saffron: saffron, chilli and herb broth 37

saffron couscous with roasted coconut and pistachios 116

salads: broad bean and carrot salad with preserved lemon 133

dried apricot and apple salad with yogurt and mint 133

grapefruit and pomegranate salad with rosewater 134

orange and date salad with chillies and preserved lemon 130

parsley, walnut and tomato salad with pomegranate syrup 129

tomato salad with green chilli and coriander 130

salt: preserved lemons 16

sesame seeds: tomato jam with cinnamon and roasted sesame seeds 136

shallots: tagine of butternut squash, shallots, sultanas and pomegranate syrup 87

tagine of yam, shallots, garlic and prunes with orange 91

smen 16

soups: chilled almond and garlic soup 38

chunky tomato soup with vermicelli and ras el hanout 32

creamy pumpkin soup with ginger and chilli honey 34

saffron, chilli and herb broth 37

spinach: chickpea and spinach tagine with yogurt 72

acknowledgments

To my mind, the most captivating thing about this book is the photography and the design so the first person I must thank is Steve Painter whose trip to Morocco for stills and props has proved invaluable and stunning. I would also like to thank Rebecca Woods for all her help and meticulous editing and, finally, to Julia Charles for taking me on board once more.